4¹⁹⁵
Ne

22⁹¹

ZAO WOU-KI

DANIEL ABADIE

ZAO WOU-KI

MARTINE CONTENSOU

EDICIONES POLÍGRAFA, S. A.

PHOTOGRAPHY CREDITS

Magnum, Bruno Barbey, 20;
Denise Colomb, 21;
Gisèle Freund, 22;
André Morain, 25;
Daniel Rabourdin, 23, 26;
François Walch, 27.

Translated by Richard-Lewis Rees

I.S.B.N.: 84-343-0571-2
Dep. Legal: B. 17.525 - 1989 (Printed in Spain)

Printed in Spain by La Polígrafa, S. A.
Parets del Vallès (Barcelona)

CONTENTS

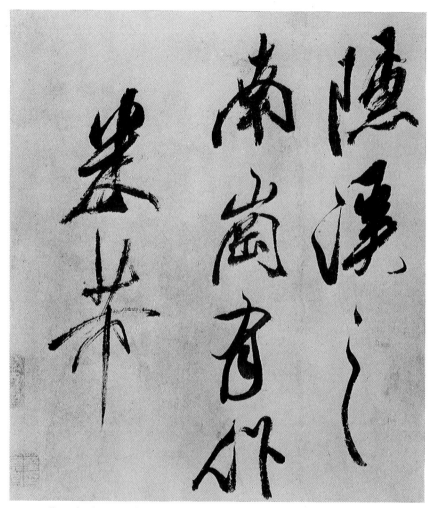

Mi-Fei calligraphy (1051-1107).

ZAO WOU-KI
by Daniel Abadie

In one of the telling and ever up-to-date reflections in *Musée imaginaire*, André Malraux reveals that our era is the first to be confronted with the art of all time and all continents. Indeed, with Gauguin painters and sculptors anxious to escape from a codified imagery apt only for official celebrations of academic art discovered the expressive richness of other civilisations and the value of what natural western cultural ethnocentrism for a long time called primitive arts. Thus the discovery of Polynesia by Gauguin, of black art by the cubists and Red Indian art by the surrealists, during their exile in North America because of the Second World War, constitute the first evidence of progressive evidence of parity between European and other cultures. In the fifties, when the West was inventing lyrical abstraction and informal art on discovering in the spontaneity of the abstract sign the image of a new liberty, the painters at the service of this new aesthetic understood, though they had made a fundamental mistake, that oriental calligraphies originated in the same spontaneous invention, in a similar impulse and in an equally decisive and certain gesture. Some painters of the period, such as Mark Tobey, had been initiated into calligraphy in the thirties, during their stay in China or Japan. They preserved — and occasionally masterfully used — the sense of the fluidity of ink, the flexibility of the wrist movement that gives nuance to the inflexion of the pen-stroke, the peremptory character of the sign executed on paper and which defines its own space. But however well they mastered the use of ink, no one could aspire to that genuine knowledge of calligraphy that affirms the meaning of things and, at the same time, offers a formula that belongs to a code which is more or less clear depending on the training of the reader. Used thus, calligraphy is a cultural phenomenon that practically cannot be transmitted.

By adopting as their own cultural forms from other civilisations, European artists were able to see what was problematic or, if you prefer, artificial in such an appropriation and, in view of plastic vocabularies that in their opinion responded naturally to their own research, they had to face up to the question of how far they were justified in using such forms. Nevertheless, some of them, precisely because they belong to two cultures, managed to demonstrate this legitimacy. Such is the case of Lam, whose partially African roots assured the authenticity of his totemic figures and, once and for

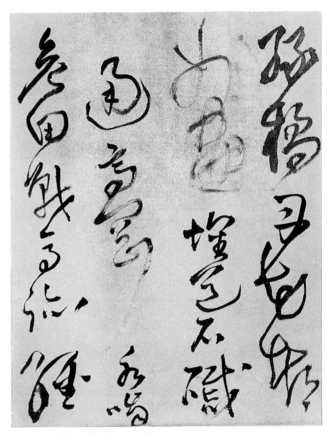

Wang-To calligraphy (1592-1652).

all, of his vision of surrealism as a whole. Similarly, Zao Wou-Ki's abstract signs have linked the most highly advanced western painting with the classical Chinese tradition. For this reason, in the prologue to a Zao Wou-Ki catalogue Manessier was able to write in 1965, "For you, brusquely, Fan K'ouan makes the same gesture as Rembrandt; Cézanne paints the same luminosity as Mi-Fu and Ni-Tsan; the great family of painters meets; the stranger becomes a brother".

However, if Zao Wou-Ki has acted as a bridge between two cultures, as a link that authenticates both the survival of a tradition and the exactitude of advanced research, it is because previously he had renounced the forms of his own culture in order to embrace the vocabulary of modern painting. In the China of the thirties, when he was studying in the School of Fine Arts of Hang-Chou, he decided to take sides with modern art, that is, western art and oil painting. Such an option did not mean for him the renunciation of the great achievments of Chinese

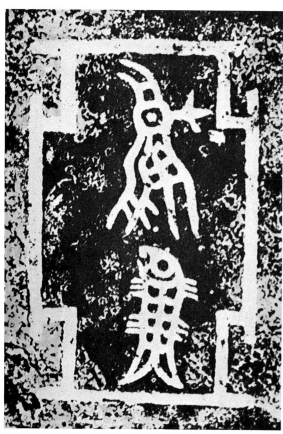

Inscription on bronze, Chang Dynasty (1766-1122 B.C.).

painting, from Mi-Fu to the Eight Eccentrics of Suzhou, but rather the certainty — contrary to the training he received — that the attempt to reproduce as ideal models the masterpieces of the past can only lead to stagnation in art. Such a rejection of an academic tradition which impressionism had savagely attacked would be unthinkable in China, where the masters of traditional art are praised precisely for their ability to faithfully reproduce the works of their predecessors. Among Chinese painters of the first half of the twentieth century, belonging to the avant-garde meant not so much revising forms as adopting oil paint, a technique foreign to the Chinese tradition, which was based on the use of ink. Furthermore, on the basis of the experience of the first Chinese painters trained in the West, Xu Bei-hong and Liu Hai-su, in China the idea spread that all oil painting, irrespective of its style, was highly modern. In consequence modernity, as defined by westerners, was limited to formulae akin, for example, to those developed by

Dunoyer de Segonzac. Indeed, the truth is that Zao Wou-Ki's best teachers at the Hang-Chou Fine Arts School, those who were most open to western influence, thought thus.

Zao Wou-Ki's initial decision to adopt oil painting is indicative of the whole spirit of his work and its evolution. Within the social context of the period, it reveals a clear awareness of the resources of western painting and the suspicion that, beyond the reproductions of impressionists, of Cézanne, Matisse and Picasso discovered in journals and books from abroad, there were possibilities before him that rule-bound traditional Chinese painting could not offer. The supremacy granted to oil painting would lead Zao Wou-Ki to regard his efforts on paper as being inferior to the main body of his work until, at the beginning of the seventies, a vast output of India-ink sketches were given the place they deserved in his *œuvre* as a whole. Then, recognised by western painters as one of their own, Zao Wou-Ki was able to allow the reappaearance of that Chinese tradition which formerly he had refused to imitate and of which from now on he could claim to be a legitimate heir.

From 1935 to 1941, during his years as a student in Hang-Chou, the adolescent determined to break with tradition thought up another affiliation based on the reproductions he saw in journals and books from abroad. As a painter he identified with the painters he copied and admired, yet he lacked the knowledge and information that would allow him to adopt a critical stance and, for the same reason, a formal freedom. Referring to his first one-man exhibition, held in 1941 on the premises of the Chino-Soviet Society in Chung-King, when the painter was twenty, he was later to say, "To be honest, the paintings I exhibited were strongly influenced by Matisse and Picasso. My Harlequins evoked Picasso's blue period; my women-statues his Greek period." However, though these painters were the inevitable references of the then avant-garde, Zao Wou-Ki was perfectly aware that there is no more liberty in copying modern masters than copying the ancients. The power of invention, which no amount of training can teach and which in his case was yet to materialise, appeared nevertheless in the drawings of his young sister Wou-She, seven years of age, as he himself confesses. At first he kept her drawings before attempting to incorporate the liberty of their graphics in canvases such as *The young bride* (1941). On doing so,

Fan K'ouan
(early tenth-century).
*Waterfall in an autumn
wood.* Paint on silk,
71¼×39¼ in.
(181×99.5 cm).
Taipei Imperial Palace
Collection.

9

he discovered the fundamental intuitiveness of the work of Paul Klee — which he was not to come to know until 1945 — and Jean Dubuffet, whose first attempts in this field were not to be presented until 1943. But where some, more mature and sure of their plastic technique, were able to situate the very essence of their work, Zao Wou-Ki presents no more than the first appearance of a more linear concept of the painting, of a style of drawing closer to the pictogram than to a descriptive search, of a poetic, rather than a narrative, vison of reality. As from 1949, these were to be some of the essential characteristics of his work.

Nevertheless, until then the painter was to multiply projects and contradictory attitudes, ever searching in the formulae of western painting or ancient Chinese art — at that time the artist showed an interest in prints from the Han period that was to be revealed in the works that in 1946 he exhibited in Shanghai — solutions to the two major problems that concerned him: the invention of a kind of drawing free from all academicism and the plastic use of a colour which, as he himself was to say in his conversations with Pierre Schneider, had ceased to exist in China in the fifteenth century. In Paris, where he arrived on April 1 1948, he was at last to find the original solution that would take his painting out from its phase of preparatory search and allow him to produce his first finished works. It is worth asking oneself whether perhaps it was not the sudden confrontation with the body of western art that was to allow Zao Wou-Ki, an assiduous visitor both to the Louvre and to avant-garde exhibitions, to find through contrast the characteristic forms of his first period. As from 1950, what was to interest specialists and art lovers was his use of delicate colour, treated more often in terms of nuances and assonances rather than of contrasts, together with cobweb-like graphics that seem to irrigate the whole surface of the canvas. The split between drawing and colour, which becomes increasingly subtle the more in the same work both elements alternately predominate as if in a musical composition with a dominant tone at each moment, provided thus a new solution to the eternal dilemma of content and form. Indeed, the experiment of lithography in colour which Zao Wou-Ki undertook in 1950, in which the work emerges from the superimposition of different-coloured plates, is not very far removed from the concept of a work that makes simultaneous use of loose elements and the transparency of colour in order to achieve unity. Until then, seduced by the novelty of oil paint, Zao Wou-Ki had used it often with a lavishness that, although rarely becoming impasto, nevertheless retained the imprint of each one of his brush-strokes. By contrast as from 1950 the paint was applied as a fine film on the grain of the canvas, revealing at certain points its structure and thus giving the impression that the colour did not cover it completely and the support had absorbed it, as if it were a very old work. This tendency towards archaicism was characteristic of the time. Indeed, the painters of the Paris School attempted to return to the great periods of French painting, for while some analysed the structures of Romanesque architecture (Soulages) or the enamels of Limousin (Lapicque), others became passionately interested in the frescoes of Tavant (Bazaine) and Gothic stained glass windows (Manessier) as if, beyond the tradition of the Renaissance and its concept of perspective, what they were attempting was to make renewed contact with an art that had never known academic decadence. In the case of Zao Wou-Ki, this desire to return to original sources had to be expressed differently. Indeed, Jean Leymarie has aptly pointed out that his colours suggest the "refinement of the material and colouring", the "velvety grain" of porcelain from the Song period. As regards his drawing, executed with the point of a fine brush, that presides over his work, its narrative elements are reminiscent of the figures on the sigillate bricks of the Han dynasty, whose sketchy character is offset by the evocative power of the concise annotations.

If Zao Wou-Ki's work at this time has often been not unreasonably linked with certain canvases by Paul Klee, it is because they share the same origin. Indeed, what links them is the supremacy of drawing. The two painters shared the same taste for a stroke that seems to appear on the surface of the work, determined and vibrant, in order to collect and reproduce each and every one of the inflexions of the hand and the mind. Nevertheless, this line, which no artist in the West before Klee had dared "allow to dream" (Henri Michaux), is the same one that predominates in Chinese painting and of which Shitao says in his *Reflections on painting*: "The single brush-stroke is the root and origin of calligraphy and painting".

Paul Klee's interest in the arts of the Far East, and the interpretations he was able to make of them when they were often incomprehensible to westerners, allowed

Paul Cézanne. *On the edge of the wood.* 1900-1904.
Watercolour, 12½×19½ in. (32×49.5 cm).
H. Berggruen Collection, Paris.

Henri Matisse. *The dream.* 1935.
Oil painting, 31½×25½ in. (80×65 cm).
Private collection, New York.

Girl. 1943. India ink on Chinese paper, 10¼×8¼ in. (26×20.8 cm).
The artist's collection.

Pablo Picasso. *Pierrot.* Paris, 1901.
Gouache, 13×7½ in. (33×19 cm).

Saint-Jeoire-en-Faucigny. 1950. Watercolour, 10½×8 in. (27×20.5 cm). The artist's collection.

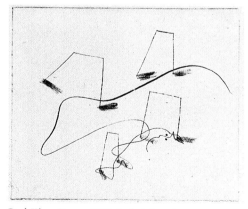

Paul Klee. *Dream.* 1930. India ink and pen, 10×12 in. (25.3×30.6 cm). Klee-Stiftung, Berne.

Zao Wou-Ki to re-examine his own past, not through the reducing filter of tradition, but rather from the distance provided by another culture. If in the forties Cézanne helped Zao Wou-Ki to "contemplate the nature of China", beyond the academic vision the other attempted to instil in him, the work of Paul Klee allowed him to rediscover his roots. From now on his culture was no longer to be a fatality, but rather a choice and a recognition. If the Swiss painter had made use of Chinese art, Zao Wou-Ki, on the contrary, returned what he had received from it: through western painting, he saw himself once again as a genuine "Chinese painter".

However, the line, as Zao Wou-Ki makes use of it in his painting, before it becomes narrative is essentially a definer of spaces. For the convergent system of western perspective he substitutes a set of multiple, off-centre focal points, joined together by a network of lines acting as vectors of tension. In his subjects, Zao Wou-Ki reproduces the metaphorical image of this system of construction that is at once stringent and imponderable: Tuscan architectures in which filled-in spaces alternate with voids; ships whose rigging seems to weave the atmosphere; mountain landscapes in which the drawing outlines, "unfaithfully exact", according to Henri Michaux's superb description, "describe the landscape without following its contours, and with little strokes like twigs breathe life into the distance". However, though all these transcriptions of space are clearly linked to ancient methods of representation, and in particular with those that use progressive upward tiering of planes, they also observe a strict respect for the flat surface of the canvas, faithful in this respect to the teachings of Cézanne. And here, once again, Zao Wou-Ki recognises his own heritage only as far as it responds to the spirit of western modernity.

Paradoxically, Zao Wou-Ki began to feel more and more comfortably integrated into the family of western painters as he progressively recovered his own culture. During his first years in Paris he had already established friendships with numerous protagonists of the European and North American avant-garde. And if, on his arrival in Paris in 1948 the young painter believed that modern art was a homogeneous whole, five years later the artist, whose international recognition was becoming ever stonger, could not overlook the great debates between the painters of his time, and more specifically the line that divided the world of art into figuration and abstraction. Although his canvases contain images that are readily identifiable, even when they are more allusive than realistic, Zao Wou-Ki identifies and exhibits with non-figurative or abstract painters, specifically those of the Galerie Pierre, to which he was committed by contract: Vieira da Silva, Mathieu, Riopelle and others. Then he inevitably had to face the question of "crossing the line", in the words of Léon Degand, between figuration and abstraction. In 1954 an event took place that can immediately be interpreted as the solution of continuity in the development of his work. With *Wind*, which he exhibits at the Salon de Mai as an indication of how important he considered the canvas, Zao Wou-Ki did away with all figurative references in his painting. This decisive moment, that for a time was to disconcert art lovers and collectors alike, was in fact the visible sign of a slow intellectual maturing process and of a deeper understanding of the problems of painting. If most of the artists of the Paris School under the term abstract art at that time practised a kind of veiled figuration that gives the painting its structure or determines its chromatic range, Zao Wou-Ki, when he adopted abstract art, set out to revise his work much more deeply. In the sense that they are codifications, and not images, of reality, the pictograms that hitherto had represented the narrative elements of his painting could not bear, as simple figurative representation, a supplementary degree of abstraction. Thus it was the graphic system of his work, which had previously been its most obvious aspect, that suddenly disappeared from his canvases when the painter decided to suppress all allusions to reality. Another repercussion here was that colour, which so far had seemed to radiate out from lines of tension in the composition — "colour appears as an occasional herald, an almost semi-nomadic element", writes René Char —, now demanded to be given a more prominent role, namely that of structuring the painting.

In *Wind* and subsequent canvases, Zao Wou-Ki's painting becomes structured on the basis of coloured masses; in fact, as soon as he embraces abstraction he becomes closer in this point to certain North American painters than to his European contemporaries. But while the American painters advocated above all the physical presence of colour, its covering or impregnating power, its materiality, Zao Wou-Ki was concerned more with the resources it offers to evoke space, to become translated into light. For this reason, the calligrapher's fine round brush

is replaced by large, flat brushes. A significant embracing of a new concept of painting that was to lead the artist progressively to increase the format of his canvases and to use no longer the loose, delicate wrist movement but to bring his whole arm, and soon even the whole body, into play.

In order to undergo such a radical change, Zao Wou-Ki had to fall back on inner resources. If the canvas ceases to be the emblematic image of the visual experience, can the painter cover it with a gesture that will be more than mere gesticulation, theatricality of painting? Although many abstract painters look towards the East and see in the spontaneity of its calligraphy the model for their own liberty, Zao Wou-Ki knows that in reality this brings with it a set of very strict rules and above all a precise meaning which is in fact the *raison d'être* of the apparently most spontaneous sign. The disassociation between the form and the meaning, which western artists cheerfully practise through ignorance, is forbidden him; for this reason he must return to characters, also charged with meaning but which are equally illegible. Ancient Chinese scripts, engraved upon bone and occasionally on certain bronze pieces — exponents of magic or religious preoccupations and yet undecipherable — are for Zao Wou-Ki references to an urge to transcend writing, the sign anterior to meaning that searched for gestural abstraction. "Their engraved appearance", observes François Cheng, "with their highly refined strokes, corresponds to the incisive traits of the painter and his need to explore forms at once sensitive and stylised". Thus, the characters that appear in the smudges of colour in *Wind* belong to no known script or vocabulary. Only Zao Wou-Ki's Chinese origin and his intimate knowledge of the principles of calligraphy give them that genuine character, that appearance of naturalness.

Doubtlessly aware that, though reinvented, these characters applied to the margin of a painting — in the same way that Chinese sages completed with poems and commentaries the image painted on a scroll — possessed an exotic charm, Zao Wou-Ki made the effort from now on to integrate them progressively into his paintings, reconsidering their spatial layout and varying their scale until they became an integral part of the body of the work, finally breaking the dichotomy between content and form, drawing and colour, that had characterised his work so far. The modification of the very body of the painting took Zao Wou-Ki from a static concept of painting

— that of the sign inscribed on a surface with no mobility other than its own vibrancy — to a dynamic vision in which the sign gradually becomes a gesture.

During an initial period, from 1954 until the beginning of the sixties, this constant research into the resources of painting was dominated by the use of chiaroscuro, a solution that was specifically western and that, simply by playing with colour, reintroduced into the work the sensation of depth and the expressiveness that disappeared with figuration. Inevitably evoking *the combat between day and night*, chiaroscuro possesses by nature a dramatic dimension which in the hitherto serene work of Zao Wou-Ki corresponds both to a period of personal troubles and to an extension of his vision, in which natural phenomena impose themselves upon the world modelled by the hand of man — cities of Italy, ports in England and Holland — which constituted the main subject of figurative canvases. This universe, which of necessity is seen in chiaroscuro, between light and shade, led the painter, in his desire to avoid a three-dimensional illusionism contrary to the teaching of Cézanne, to place the dark, heavy elements in the top or the centre of the canvas, thus intuitively restoring the principle of tiering in Chinese landscape painting, in which the mass of mountains floats at the top of the composition in order to evoke distance. On doing this, Zao Wou-Ki introduced into his work the essential role of caesura and void which, as from 1962, was decisively to determine the spirit of his paintings. The use, with abstract ends in view, of the composition principles of Chinese landscape painting — "His paintings have kept a family feeling with nature", says Henri Michaux — has often led people to view his work as if emanating from an abstract form of landscape painting. If until 1959 certain titles — *The fire, Clouds, Abandoned garden*, etc. — seem to authorise such an interpretation, it would be difficult to attribute the same naturalistic dimension to his later works, if only because of their thoroughly invented chromatism. In the same way that his *Water-lilies* breaks away from the vision of landscape offered by Monet's work, around 1960 a change took place in the body of Zao Wou-Ki's work: colour was no longer memory or evocation; it became pure plastic invention.

In a work which has now acquired all the elements necessary for its proper function, and which from now on unfolds naturally, it is difficult to mark stages. However, his leaving Paris — in 1957 Zao Wou-Ki left France for a then indefinite stay in New York — possibly originated one of the most important, if not *the* most important, mutations in his work. Indeed, it was on his return to Paris at the end of 1959 when his formats became considerably larger and, above all, when in his paintings chiaroscuro gave place to a much more effective use of colour. From this moment onwards, his painting no longer attempted to suggest a world or a confrontation of forces, but rather the exact place where this confrontation takes place, and Zao Wou-Ki would no longer give his works titles — except in the *Homages* to some of his idols — but simply the date when they were painted. In a spectacular way, *Homage to Edgar Varèse* (1964), the largest canvas he had hitherto painted, offers the image of an uproar in which, within a still illuminist environment, there is a persistence of brush-strokes, splashes, impastoes, sprayings and *grattages* in the paste, in the manner of the score of *Déserts*, in which elements of electronic music recall the material quality of the universe of sound which, by contrast, gives a classical character to the musical part treated in a traditional way. Indeed, the progressive emergence of the painterly gesture, the rejection of illusionism, characteristic of the works of the sixties and early seventies, are by no means alien to his distance from the Paris School, into which Zao Wou-Ki had integrated so naturally at first, or to the impact he had received from a kind of American painting that was not so eager to produce studio recipes such as the physical evidence of the painting. But if Zao Wou-Ki then felt closer to the American painters by virtue of the width of their objectives and the techniques employed to contribute to this, he similarly evoked the Chinese painters praised by Segalen and who literally threw themselves into the paint.

The long journey through oil painting, which Zao Wou-Ki has mastered for over thirty years — to the point that his Chinese origins are no longer considered to be the main characteristic of his work —, finally permitted the artist, in the early seventies, to tackle the repressed part of his tradition, that of ink and the brush. (Zao Wou-Ki has always made India-ink sketches but, independently of his successes in this field, he has always presented it as a secondary aspect of his work.) If hitherto all the periods of development of the painter had evolved according to the resources that he had found in his own tradition, he had not succeeded in making the transition represented by the use of oil paint guarantee for him a new conquest, rather than a step backwards. This time, on using ink and brushes, Zao Wou-Ki inevitably took up the Chinese tradition and placed it face-to-face with the modern language it had failed to create for itself. Zao Wou-Ki's wash drawings therefore became, when he began work on a first group in 1971, not a pastime secondary to the main body of his painting, but its culmination. The freedom gained over nearly twenty years of practice in the field of abstract art now found two exemplary allies in the fluidity of ink and the instantly recovered deftness of his wrist. His understanding of abstract art allowed the painter to take advantage of the imponderables relative to ink — more or less rapid absorption by the paper, smudges and spattering —, while the virtuosity of the calligrapher assured him perfect control over the main effects.

The wash drawings, to which Zao Wou-Ki periodically returned in subsequent years, are the catalysts of an essential notion in his painting, the notion of emptiness. As the painter himself points out, "one brush-stroke is enough" to make the white of the paper, its reserve, vibrate. Thus, with the sole quality of the support lit up by the ink, those areas of tension materialise, empty of events, which have always been an essential element in his work. From his figurative paintings, in the work of Zao Wou-Ki graphics has always respected the presence of areas of colour that ensure the plastic function of the canvas and prevent it from becoming a mere drawing with highlights in colour. Later, in the abstract works, is when by virtue of a phenomenon of intersticial spaces and caesuras, a tension is created between signs. This active void, a fundamental concept in Chinese thought, was given pride of place in the paintings contemporary with and subsequent to the drawings in India ink. In the most notable of these, the graphic elements seem to have been pushed right to the edges of the work, by the frame, so that with the vibration only of colour, nuanced and animated by tiny events, the skin of the canvas can better be covered.

Zao Wou-Ki in the seventies extended this spatial game to a monumental scale. "Painting", he says, "is a struggle between the canvas and myself, a physical struggle. Above all in the large formats, which allow more human gestures, a genuine projection. One must become completely immersed". The triptych was to be the privileged support for such realisations, its very nature

Piazza. 1950. Oil on canvas, 57½×38¼ in. (146×97 cm). Musée national d'art moderne, Paris.

The oracle's bone. 1339-1281 B.C. Engraved tortoise shell, 6 in. (15 cm) long.

Wash drawing, 1974. 10×6½ in. (25.3×16.5 cm).
Page from the artist's album.

offering in the continuum of its reading, the caesura of its double articulation. Thus, the artist is able to make use of composition in order to refute the solutions of continuity and to invent a rhythm that unifies the work as a whole or, on the contrary, seek support in these solutions and introduce in the development of the work points of reference that order the painting in masses of colour, in the same way that contemporary musicians order the sound mass. This interplay of dissonances, this constant examination of the norms of composition, are often accentuated by a very free and daring use of colour, ranging from light-coloured camaieus to much more strident, radical colours. Thus to oil painting, whose resources seemed to have been codified and refined by five centuries of activity in the West, Zao Wou-Ki, after long experimentation was able to give back the capacity of invention and perturbation that is characteristic of discovery.

A painter is someone with a constant obsession. Commentators often look in his work for traces of a philosophical quest, whereas his work is almost invariably the material result of the need to solve a plastic problem. In Zao Wou-Ki's case, and this initial intuition has become consolidated and clarified with each new period in his painting, the obsession has been to give a modern view of that particular space of Chinese painting — when it seemed to be caught in the grip of academicism —, and to write for this tradition the new chapter it was unable to produce for itself. To achieve this, Zao Wou-Ki has had to face all risks and verify, against his own tradition, through the use of oil paint, abstraction, intense colours, what was universal in this tradition. Zao Wou-Ki has had to rediscover in his own field the mystical experience, that experience that consists in losing oneself in order to find oneself again later. Then, in that "orchard of signs" that Henri Michaux evoked at the beginning, he has been able, little by little, to mature what according to Lao Tseu is the end of the Road: the *Great painting without image*.

Wash drawing, 1971. 24½×19¼ in. (62.5×49 cm).
Alex Maguy collection, Paris.

Wou-Chi (who died at the age of 5), his sister
Wou-Hwa (who died in 1939), his brother Wu-Wai
and Wou-Ki at the age of 6, in Nang-Tung, 1927.

Granfather Tsao.

LIFE INTO WORK

by Martine Contensou

Zao Wou-Ki was born in Peking in 1921, but he spent his childhood in Nantung, to the north of Shanghai, together with his five younger brothers and sisters. Each year, on the day of the family's ancestors, whose genealogy goes back to the Song dynasty, his eyes contemplated the ritual displaying of the family treasure, composed of precious objects and two paintings. Through one of these, by the eleventh-century poet and landscape painter Mi-Fu, the boy discovered both painting and calligraphy which, emerging from the same brush, constituted a double art, conceived to create "a mediumnical space in which real life becomes actualised".*

His family environment favoured the rapid development of his talent in his acquiring these two languages. His father, who alongside his activities as a banker also painted, tried to show him the beauty in everyday objects converted into works of art, while transmitting to him the words of the *Tao Te King* referring to the fundamental notion of Chinese thought, that of emptiness: "Clay is modelled to make vessels, but their use depends upon the empty space inside". His grandfather, a wise Taoist and an extraordinary personality, was not content merely to recount his adventures as an infantryman in the Manchu Empire, but also taught him to read and write, and would draw on the back of every character the corresponding image. One of his uncles, a poet and teacher of Chinese literature, stimulated his taste for letters and history. Another initiated him into European art, bringing him back from his visits to Paris postcards with reproductions of masterpieces, among these Proud'hon's Allegories and Millet's *Angelus*. For her part, his mother anxiously watched how her son would bedaub her white porcelain plates with colour, but she put up no objections when at the age of fourteen he decided to leave the warmth of the lovely family home, built in a modernist style at the request of the father, to study at the School of Fine Arts in Hang-Chou.

> But let us direct our gaze for the last time towards that round opening inside which the moon of the eighth month will come to be framed, beside the mirror that detains time and which has been placed at our feet to reflect and assimilate, through the fleeting accusations of shade and colour, substance.
>
> P. Claudel, *Hang-Tchéou*

---

* F. Cheng, *Vide et Plein, le langage pictural chinois*, Éd. du Seuil, 1979.

Thus, Claudel left the Western lake beside Hang-Chou ten years before Zao Wou-Ki reached the city, in 1935, to begin his art studies in the middle of this very lake, where the school forms an artificial island with its pavilions built on stilts.

After waiting a while for reasons of age, Zao Wou-Ki passed the entrance examination to the school, where he was to spend six years in an atmosphere he described as "exactly the same as the one la Toscana knew, among the cypresses at the time of the Italian primitives".

In the morning the students learnt the techniques and principles of western painting and acquired knowledge of absolutely academic concepts: perspective, anatomy, drawing with plaster figures and, later with live models. During the final year they were initiated into oil painting, but Zao Wou-Ki could not wait so long to begin studying a subject so alien to traditional Chinese painting, which all the students studied in the afternoon, being taught from the very first year how to handle ink and watercolour. At home he painted landscapes and portraits of his little sister. Impatient to break out from the straitjacket of a fossilized tradition, he turned back to Chinese art prior to the fourteenth century, to Song ceramics that he admired for the refinement and colouring of its raw material, and to the painter-poets whose landscapes he would later discover *in vivo* when crossing the rivers and mountains of Ssu-Chuan when, during the Sino-Japanese war, the students had to be evacuated from Hang-Chou and sought shelter in Tchouang King.

It was here that, leafing through North-American journals, he discovered the work of Renoir, Cézanne, Modigliani, Matisse and Picasso in full-page, full-colour reproductions.

During this period — 1941-1942 —, when he was appointed auxiliary teacher at the school where he had trained, Zao Wou-Ki organised the first exhibition of his works, strongly influenced, in his own words, by Matisse and Picasso, and then a second exhibition of the work of young Chinese artists — including himself — who were attempting to break away from tradition.

> We bring facility with us when we are born. This must be eliminated; it is the death of art.
>
> Cézanne

"Cézanne opened the way for me; thanks to him, I've learnt to see with my own eyes", says Zao Wou-Ki. Like

Professor Lin's daughter, his second sister, the architect Won-Ten, his mother, his father, Lan-Lan and their children, the artist, his youngest brother and his third sister before departing for Paris on 26-2-1948 on the packet steamer André Lebon.

China, pavilion on the water in Hang-Chou.
Photo: Bruno Barbey.

the master of Aix, he did not run away from this critical moment, the first moment of art "our own dawn above nothingness", that begins to break as his decision to travel to Europe gathers strength.

He sailed from Shanghai, with his wife Lan-Lan, on February 26 1948, and disembarked in Marseilles thirty-six days later. He marvelled at the light of Provence, so dear to Van Gogh, and as soon as he arrived in Paris he hurried to the Louvre. Egypt and Ancient Greece fascinated him. Cimabue's *Maestà* sent him into raptures of admiration: "It's the most beautiful thing in the Louvre. That serenity: everything is almost on the same level, but the golden halos create a strange perspective, on planes. This recalls to me old Chinese landscapes, in which the planes are separated by curtains of mist". He admired Cranach, Uccello, Mantegna. He stopped before Watteau, Chardin, Goya, Titian, Rembrandt, Vermeer and Poussin, of whom he says, "He's a poet! What charm! This is the joy of painting".

Zao Wou-Ki shared the same fervent joy with a considerable number of artists who arrived in Paris between 1946 and 1948 and who very quickly became "lifelong friends": Sam Francis, Riopelle, Soulages, Hartung, Nicolas de Staël, Vieira da Silva, and others, whom he met in those meeting and confrontation places that were the Galerie de Nina Dausset and the Galerie Pierre.

After sojourns in different Montparnasse hotels, he finally settled in a small studio in the Rue du Moulin-Vert. He learned French, he explored the city, museums and galleries, he went to concerts... At the Académie de la Grande-Chaumière, whose guiding spirit was then Othon Friesz, he developed a passion for the nude. During these months of acclimatisation his painting was held in abeyance, but he drew very much. Furthermore, he became initiated into several copper engraving procedures and, having discovered the road to the Desjobert printing works, he became an enthusiast of the technique of lithography. The surprising series of eight colour plates he completed in 1949 immediately suggested to Michaux a poetic commentary imbued with the same spirit as a Chinese poem inscribed on a picture, in which "he genuinely inhabits the space by introducing there a living dimension, that of Time".[*]

---

[*] Bernard Lamblin, *Peinture et Temps*, Éd. Cercle d'Art, Paris, 1983.

Jean-Paul Riopelle, Germain, Vieira da Silva, Pierre Loeb, Georges Mathieu and Zao Wou-Ki
at the Galerie Pierre in 1952. Photo: Denise Colomb.

From this first contact between the work of the painter and that of the poet — who, won over by Chinese painting was also to become a painter himself — an unfailing friendship grew up between the two men. From this brilliant fusion emerged the profound originality of a work which, over and above any discourse, invokes poetry, the only element capable of elucidating it by transposing its rhythms into words, its spaces into silences, its colours into music.

> If we see in his work a technique close to that of a modern western artist, this is not in detriment to his traditional Chinese roots, similar to the murmur of his mother tongue, a road that proceeds from authority.

> H. Michaux

In the prologue to the catalogue for Zao Wou-Ki's exhibitions in London and New York in 1952, Michaux reveals this "Chinese road" in the graphic strokes that characterised his work at the time — reminiscent of the archaic inscriptions engraved on divining bones and ritual bronzes of the Chang dynasty —, a way opening towards abstraction, since the meanings they still contain appear to be on the point of vanishing.

"So I am 'abstract with memories'", writes Paul Klee in his *Diary* of 1915; Klee, who himself had studied the ways of Chinese painting in an attempt to respond to "chaos" with Rhythm, crossed frontiers of space and time, becoming reunited with one of Zao Wou-Ki's favourite painters, Shitao, a Taoist monk who, in his *Reflections*

Henri Michaux. 1964. Photo: Gisèle Freund.

on painting, published in 1731, wrote, "The brush serves to bring things out of chaos".

In 1951, while in Berne on the occasion of his exhibition of engravings, Zao Wou-Ki discovered the work of Klee which, in his opinion, has many points of contact with his own. Indeed, some of his 1950 canvases such as *Arezzo, Piazza* and *Boats*, in which Zao Wou-Ki reconstructs from memory the landscapes and cities of Italy, a country he has just visited, reveal strong affinities with the work of the German painter. "Figurative aspects subsist in my paintings until 1953", he says. "But I have always proceeded according to a kind of pictographic condensation, limiting images to their structures."

At this time Zao Wou-Ki travelled widely, visiting Tuscany, Rome, Pompei, Naples, Ischia and, in 1952, Spain. Travelling, at once rupture and opening, constituted for him a pretext for reconciliation, an element of equilibrium. As from 1950 he exhibited regularly at the Salon de Mai, the Galerie Pierre, with which he had signed a contract until 1957, in the United States, Switzerland, and London, among others.

His paintings had found a ready market. Lyrical abstraction, practised by the friends he had made soon after arriving in Paris, was at the height of fashion. However, although he collected works by Vieira da Silva, Hartung, Soulages, Schneider and Bazaine, he kept himself apart from the currents then prevalent on the artistic scene.

A question of conscience began to obsess him: "Is it still painting that poses problems for me, or is it the subject that imposes itself on me?"

In 1954 Zao Wou-Ki launched himself into the world of abstract painting: "During this period my painting became illegible. I was moving towards imaginary, undecipherable writing". In the works from previous years, elements from nature had already become transformed into signs, but the transfer from the figure to abstraction took place also thanks to a technical change: the substitution of round brushes for rectangular, flat-ended brushes that permitted the application of a thicker, more fluid coat of paint and gave more space to the flourish and more time to rhythm. The first work to be produced during this period bears the significant title of *Wind*. For two years his dealer, Pierre Loeb, was unable to sell his works. "The public wasn't buying, but I stuck to my guns", recalls Zao Wou-Ki, remembering those fascinating, though difficult, times.

One must work with ease of movement, the hand held high, and the brush-stroke will be capable of brusque metamorphoses. When the wrist is guided by the soul, rivers and mountains surrender their souls.

Shitao, *Reflections on painting*

Zao Wou-Ki handled his new brushes with the ease of a supreme master, in the spirit of Chinese discipline. His mastery of western techniques was increasing, and he practised them according to the rules prescribed by Shitao and an ancient author whom he frequently quotes: "The wrist, as the prolongation of the free arm, must move with the same suppleness as the neck of the goose, in order to transmit the flow of inner life". He worked without an easel, leaning the canvas on the wall or stretching it out on the floor, like Chinese painters who compose their horizontal or vertical scrolls placing them on the floor or on a low table and working from right to left and from top to bottom. "This direct way of immersing oneself in the work, of becoming merged with the work itself, is one of the characteristics of abstract painting of an organic or informal tendency, which then becomes widespread the whole world over and acquires in the United States the original, powerful dimension of *action painting*", notes Jean Leymarie.*

However, unlike Pollock, leader of the *action painting* movement, Zao Wou-Ki did not paint his pictures with rapid strokes. He used a continual flourish with which to make his compositions.

Between 1954 and 1957, between *Wind* and *Mistral*, his formats become larger and his canvases are stretched horizontally or vertically almost as far as breaking point, or else become vast rectangles with imprecise edges. Continuing his "unique dialogue with Chinese scrolls" (A. Malraux), his work invites us in turn "to a veritable temporal mobilisation of our concept of space".**

The close relationship between this work and music was reinforced by the painter's friendship with Edgar Varèse, whom he met in 1955. While painting, Zao Wou-Ki listened to Bach and Mozart or sang to himself arias from his favourite operas. He also liked modern composers such as Debussy, Bartok, Satie and Webern. He was one of the first members of *Domaine musical*, an association founded in the autumn of 1954 by Boulez to initiate people into an appreciation of the new forms of composition and the execution of serial music. At the end of the same year Varèse returned to Paris, after an absence of twenty years, for the presentation of *Déserts* at the Théâtre des Champs-Elysées. "Still today I remember the performance of *Déserts*", says Zao Wou-Ki. "This desert, which is at once physical and moral, in its sonorous paroxysm translates a vision of the world that has never ceased to obsess me. As from that moment, I began to give rhythm to light, following other pulsations".

In *Déserts* the silence is as important as emptiness in Zao Wou-Ki's canvases, an infinitely worked surface, a source of light and vibrations and, in accordance with Chinese thought, "the place, par excellence, where transformations take place, where Fullness can achieve its true plenitude".***

The studio in Rue Jonquoy, Paris.

With Arpad Szènes and Vieira da Silva. 1973.
Photo: D. Rabourdin.

* Jean Leymarie, *Zao Wou-Ki*, Éd. Cercle d'Art, Paris, 1986.
** B. Lamblin, *op. cit.*
*** F. Cheng, *op. cit.*

In May 1957 the artist presented his first one-man exhibition, the fruit of prolific creation, at the Galerie de France. But it was at this time that he went through a deep crisis that forced him to separate from Lan-Lan, his companion since the age of sixteen. Works such as *Before the storm, Black crowd, Torn mountain, The fire,* and *We two* reveal the uncontainable pressure that life exercised on his work then.

In September Zao Wou-Ki decided to go on a journey of indefinite duration. He went first to New York, where he met up with his brother, the composer Varèse and one of his first admirers, the architect I.M. Pei, whose family in China was on friendly terms with his own. A defender of the vitality of American painting, he met several of its most outstanding representatives who immediately become his friends: Kline, Guston, Marca-Relli, Gottlieb and Baziotes, along with Samuel Kootz, an art connoisseur who was to be his dealer for seven years, until he closed his gallery in 1967.

After his sojourn in New York, Zao Wou-Ki travelled with his friends Pierre and Colette Soulages to Washington, Chicago and San Francisco, whose Chinatown he explored. He visited every museum, was surprised by the number of French works they contain and he commented with Soulages on his reaction to those that attracted his attention. Together they went to the islands of Hawaii, then to Japan and they parted in Hong Kong, where Zao Wou-Ki stayed for six months. Here he met May, whom he married, and the couple then travelled to Thailand, Greece and Italy before returning to Paris in August 1958.

The annual presentation of his works at the Kootz Gallery in New York allowed him to maintain and consolidate his friendships on the other side of the Atlantic.

At the end of 1959, back again in Paris, Zao Wou-Ki bought a house in the Rue Jonquoy. A small garden separated the house from a depôt in which the architect Georges Johannet was to build him a studio shut off from the outside world and lit from the roof. This quiet, hidden-away studio was to be his place of work henceforth.

Breathe! Invisible poem
pure perpetual interchange of the being to me that belongs
with the space of the world
in which I become myself rhythmically
… Single wave of which I am the successive sea.

R. M. Rilke, *Sonnets to Orpheus*

As from 1958 Zao Wou-Ki's work, now more ethereal, developed like a scansion of time. The graphic traces that people it breathe; the almost volatile colours vibrate. The titles have disappeared giving place to simple dates indicating the day when the painting was completed. In 1961, in answer to a question, the painter declared: "If the influence of Paris is undeniable in the whole of my artistic development, I must also say that I have been rediscovering China as my personality has become consolidated. In my recent canvases, this is expressed innately. Paradoxically, it is to Paris that I owe my return to my deepest roots". One year later he illustrated with ten lithographs one of Malraux first books, *La tentation de l'Occident*, the confrontation between two cultures in which he moved. Thanks to the help of the writer, who was then Minister of Culture, Zao Wou-Ki obtained French nationality in 1964.

Zao Wou-Ki's work as an illustrator continued through the years with poetic texts by Rimbaud, Saint-John Perse, René Char, Jean Lescure, Jean Laude and Roger Caillois.

His paintings are exhibited in Paris, Grenoble, New York, Madrid, Florence, Tokyo and elsewhere. Becoming increasingly well-known, Zao Wou-Ki, whose creative capacity continues to grow, works in the solitude of his studio while seeking the company of his all-time friends and giving up his journeys of exploration. May, whose health has always been delicate, falls ill increasingly often. The painter, concerned by this, seeks refuge in his work, into which he pours the tensions that are oppressing him. His brush-strokes knot together convulsively in black masses that dominate the surface while from his dark shades in confrontation with each other a clearing occasionally emerges.

Zao Wou-Ki completed this series of paintings with his *Homage to Edgar Varèse* (25-10-64), a canvas of large dimensions (255×345 cm.) finished a few months before the composer's death.

I paint large canvases because I want to create a state of intimacy. A large painting implies an immediate interchange: you become integrated into it.

Mark Rothko

In 1964 Zao Wou-Ki began to adopt formats that, by their proportions, respond to the amplitude of a gesture impatient to create new harmonic relationships. "Painting", he says, "is a struggle between the canvas and myself, a physical struggle". He gave himself up totally to this exchange, which he compared to the battles that take place on a tennis court. And when in 1967 the exhibition at the Galerie de la France gathered in thirty paintings the fruits of the last four years, the essayist and critic P. Schneider wrote: "Instead of absorbing the gesture, the background is more and more punished by it. The effervescence that the intermediate areas had initially gained has now invaded the whole painting. A wide, irresistible movement crosses it from side to side".

Recently the painter had begun to travel once more: in 1964 he went to Amsterdam to contemplate again the works of Vermeer and Rembrandt; then New York, where he renewed contact with his friend I. M. Pei; in 1965, Vienna, where he was able to admire the works of Bruegel and present a retrospective exhibition of his graphic work; in 1967 he went to Dublin, where he met the American painter Barnett Newman, whose work he admired as much as that of Rothko or Pollock. Of Barnett Newman, whom he would later often visit in the United States, Zao Wou-Ki says: "We have undoubtedly been very close to one another; linked by a great friendship and points of view in common, perhaps". The same year he wrote, in collaboration with Claude Roy, his first biographer since 1957, a book on Han prints (209 B.C. to 200 A.D.). In 1969 more travels took him from Canada to the United States and then to Mexico. Here he stayed at the house of the painter Tamayo, a friend of his, and he visited the archaeological sites, which impressed him deeply.

In 1970, during the festival of Salzburg, he directed an artistic seminar in the city, Mozart's little homeland. That same year Claude Roy's monograph was reprinted, with a prologue in which Henri Michaux says:

Zao Wou-Ki has also abandoned the concrete.
But his paintings have preserved a familiar air with Nature.
(...) Nature captured in the mass.
(...) Empty of trees, of rivers, without woods or hills, but full of waterspouts, of quakes, of lighting, of impulses of flows, of vaporous coloured magmas that dilate, rise up, explode. Called away by new problems, by dramas, by encroachments.
(...) Through nature, in alliance with her, it is possible to live more intensely than when living alone.
(...) Nature, taken in all her extension, her depth. It will be possible to live on another scale.
In Zao Wou-Ki's paintings, of gigantic dimensions, in proportion to the extent of his feelings, there are — magnifying transfer —

Zao Wou-Ki and Claude Roy.
Photo: André Morain.

In Mexico with Olga and Rufino Tamayo and his cousin.

ever increasingly powerful assumptions of earth. Enormous masses, when the time comes, must gain height. This nature recreates for Zao Wou-Ki a splendid geological period.

Here predominate levitations, mixing, upheaval.

It is well-known that Zao Wou-Ki's canvases have a particular virtue: they are beneficent.

One year later, May's illness took a turn for the worse. The artist, unable to paint, returned to the technique of wash drawings whose rules he had known since childhood, but which he had not used so far through fear of being carried away by what is easy. Once again it was Henri Michaux who, foreseeing the future that this speciality offers, evokes his "ink games":

> Once the black is applied, the white of the paper, absent here and there is awoken in unexpected areas. It is the emptiness that, for the harmony of the World, must never be absent; it does not matter where.
>
> (...) Abstraction takes its place
> abstract through detatchment
> purification of presences.
> (...) With the suppleness of silk
> a landing on a beach of paper
> gravity has vanished.

With Hans Hartung. 1973. Photo: D. Rabourdin.

In the canvases that Zao Wou-Ki painted in 1971, as well as those begun previously and completed now, and which bear the two dates of execution, appear transparent blacks which are the product of his experience with wash drawings.

May died on March 10, 1972. Since 1963, despite the illness that was causing her to waste away, she had secretly been producing a series of sculptures. In homage to her, the Galerie de France exhibited them in November alongside Zao Wou-Ki's wash drawings.

On March 25 Zao Wou-Ki returned to China after an absence of twenty-four years. He visited the tomb of his father, who had died in 1968, and then went to see his mother, with whom he travelled to Peking, Shanghai and Hang-Chou, the places where he had spent his childhood.

With Eillen and I.M. Pei. 1976.

> It matters little whether art is figurative or, as some people say, abstract. Genuine art is not content merely to replace images with signs; it simply proposes signs that are configured and surpassed by the gesture of form.

H. Maldiney, *Regard Parole Espace*

Back in France, Zao Wou-Ki completed *May, in memoriam* (10-9-72), a vast field of transfiguration wrested from the void, whose light evokes, by virtue of its intensity, the penultimate poem of *Connaissance de l'Est*, which Claudel titles *L'heure jaune* (The yellow hour):

This is the yellowest hour of the whole year! (...) The golden time comes in which everything is transmuted, in the heavens and on Earth.

In autumn 1973 Zao Wou-Ki took up his activities once again. In 1975 an exhibition at the Galerie de France presented their fruits: fifteen oil paintings, some of very large dimensions. The canvases reveal the recovery of his creative force, his having met and subsequently married Françoise Marquet doubtless having contributed much to this. In the preface to the catalogue, René Char wrote a poetical text, *Le dos houleux du miroir* (The hostile back of the mirror), that attempts to capture in its modulations the ebb and flow of this energy.

In February 1975, Zao Wou-Ki had to return to Shanghai to be beside his mother, who was very ill. Months earlier together they had visited Su-Chou, his native city, famous for its gardens in which the wise Song used to gather.

1975 and 1976 are years of intense activity marked by canvases of very large format and crowned by the triptych titled *Homage to Malraux*. He also experiments with smaller dimension canvases: the rhythm is concentrated increasingly in the "inner emptiness", where the vibration of the being can be felt. "Emptiness lives inside all things, in the very heart of their substance and their mutation", wrote Lao Tseu six centuries before our era.

Zao Wou-Ki in his studio. Photo: François Walch.

As the years go by, his colours become increasingly lavish and daring, and the work of Zao Wou-Ki is shown in new exhibitions: in Tokyo, where he travels with his wife after first stopping off in New York, and in Paris, the city finally paying homage to him at the Galeries nationales du Grand Palais in 1980. Jean Leymarie, who organised the latter, chose for it "thirty canvases of large format which unfold symphonically and culminate in two sumptuous recent triptychs: one with small blue and black threads (5-6-80) and the other with an orange irradiation (24-11-80), in which the linear ramification is integrated into a space that floats in perpetual metamorphosis".

Zao Wou-Ki in his studio. June, 1988.

In this and following triptychs, as in the *Water Lilies* by Monet, whom Zao Wou-Ki admires, the outline has disappeared and the line has become pulverised. It is as if the oil paint had acquired the qualities of ink and the canvas had become paper.

The Grand Palais exhibition travelled through Japan, Hong-Kong and Singapore, which provided the artist with the opportunity to make new journeys. During these he visited China, which he showed to his wife, and he attended the opening of the magnificent hotel built by Pei on the Fragrant Hills, near Peking. Zao Wou-Ki produced two India ink panels as part of its decoration.

In 1983 his work was exhibited for the first time in his own country: in Peking and then in Hang-Chou, specifically in the school where he had studied as a boy. (Two years later the same school invited him to run a one-month seminar during the course of painting and drawing, while his wife taught art history and museography.) On the home journey he stopped in Singapore to finalise details about the site and format of the monumental painting Pei had commissioned from him for the building he was erecting in that city. The work, an exceptional triptych ten metres wide, conceived and painted throughout the summer of 1985, from June to October, will be installed in the hall of the building.

Months later, in February 1986, Zao Wou-Ki paid a splendid *Homage to Matisse*, in which he gives his own version of the *Window-Door* of 1914, on which he once commented in terms we should like to apply to his work as a whole: "In China someone might say that *Window-Door* is a magic painting, since in front of the door, empty and full at the same time, is life, dust, the air we breathe; but what is there behind? It is an immense, black space. For all of us it is a door open to true painting".

GALLERIES AND MUSEUMS CONTAINING
WORKS BY ZAO WOU-KI

AUSTRIA:
Albertina Museum, Vienna.

BELGIUM:
Bibliothèque Royale de Belgique, Brussels.
Musée des Beaux-Arts, Brussels.
Fondation Veranneman, Kruishouten.

BRAZIL:
Museu de Arte Moderna, Rio de Janeiro.

CANADA:
Canadian Imperial Bank of Commerce, Toronto.
Musée des Beaux-Arts, Montreal.

CHINA:
The Fragrant Hills Hotel, architect: Pei (near the city of Peking),
Peking.
Zyejiang Academy of Fine Arts, Hang Chou.

FINLAND:
Kunstmuseum Athenaeum, Helsinki.

FRANCE:
Musée de Valence.
Musée Ingres, Montauban.
Musée du Havre.
Musée National d'Art Moderne, Paris.
Musée d'Art Moderne de la Ville de Paris.
Fonds National d'Art Contemporain, Paris.
Bibliothèque Nationale, Paris.
Manufacture Nationale des Gobelins.
Manufacture Nationale de la Savonnerie, Paris.
Manufacture Nationale de Sèvres, Paris.
Musée Bertrand, Châteauroux.
Société des Compteurs Schlumberger, Paris.
Air France, Direction Générale, Paris.
Musée de Metz.
Total, Compagnie Française des Pétroles, Paris.
École Nationale Normale Supérieure, Lyon.
Musée d'Unterlinden, Colmar.

GERMANY:
Folkwang Museum, Essen.

HONG KONG:
Hong Kong Museum of Art.

INDONESIA:
Museum of Djakarta.

ISRAEL:
Museum of Tel-Aviv.

ITALY:
Galleria Civica d'Arte Moderna, Genova.
Galleria Civica d'Arte Moderna, Milan.
Museum of Fine Arts, Milan.

JAPAN:
Fukuoka Art Museum, Fukuoka.
Nagaoka Contemporary Art Museum, Nagaoka.
Bridgestone Museum of Art, Tokyo.
The Fuji Telecasting Co. Ltd. Collection, Tokyo.
Iwaki Museum of Contemporary Art.
Kanichiro Ishibashi Collection, Tokyo.
National Osaka Museum of Modern Art.
Nobutaka Shikanai Collection, Tokyo.
H. Imasato Collection, Tokyo.
The Hakone Open-Air Museum.
National Osaka Art Museum, Osaka.

LUXEMBOURG:
Musée d'Histoire et d'Art, Luxembourg.

MEXICO:
Museo de Arte Contemporáneo, Mexico.
Museo de Arte Moderno, Mexico.
Museo Tamayo de Arte Contemporáneo, Mexico.

PORTUGAL:
Museu Nacional das Belas Artes, Oporto.

SINGAPORE:
Raffles City. Architect: I.M. Pei.

SWITZERLAND:
Musée d'Art et d'Histoire "Fondation Gerald Cramer", Geneva.
Thyssen-Bornemisza Collection, Castagnola.

TAIWAN:
Bibliothèque Préfectorale, Tai-chung.
National Museum of History, Taipei.

UNITED KINGDOM:
The Tate Gallery, London.
Victoria and Albert Museum, London.

UNITED STATES:
Aldrich "Old 100" Collection, Ridgefield.
Art Institute of Chicago, Chicago.
Atlanta Art Center, Atlanta.
Atlanta University, Atlanta.
Berkeley University, Los Angeles.
Carnegie Institute, Pittsburgh.
Oyahoga Savings Association, Cleveland.
Cincinnati Art Museum, Cincinnati.
Coldby Museum of Art, Maine.
Detroit Institute of Art, Detroit.
Finch Art College Museum, New York.
Fogg Museum of Art, Harvard University, Cambridge
(Massachusetts).
Herbert F. Johnson Museum of Art, Ithaca (New York).
Hirshhorn Museum, Washington D.C.
International Minerals and Chemical Corporation, Stanford
(California).
Medical Research Center, Los Angeles.
Museum of Fine Arts, Houston (Texas).
The Museum of Modern Art, New York.
Museum of Modern Art, San Francisco.
Rose Museum, Brandeis University.
San Francisco Museum, San Francisco.
The Solomon R. Guggenheim Museum, New York.
Stanford University, Stanford (California).
Upjohn Company Collection, Kalamazoo (Michigan).
Virgin Island Museum, St. Thomas (Virgin Islands).
Virginia Museum of Fine Arts, Richmond (Kentucky).
University of Virginia Art Museum, Richmond (Kentucky).
Wadsworth Atheneum, Hartford (Connecticut).
White Art Museum, Cornell University, Ithaca (New York).
Walker Art Center, Minneapolis.
Yale University Art Gallery, New Haven.
High Museum of Art, Atlanta (Georgia).
Middle South Service Inc.
Asia Art Museum of San Francisco, The Avery Brundage
Collection.

YUGOSLAVIA:
Museum of Contemporary Art, Skopje.

BIBLIOGRAPHY

MONOGRAPHS

1957. ROY, Claude. *Zao Wou-Ki*, Le Musée de Poche.

1970. ROY, Claude. *Zao Wou-Ki*, Le Musée de Poche, new edition with a prologue by Henri Michaux.

1974. LAUDE, Jean. *Zao Wou-Ki*, Éd. La Connaissance, Brussels.

1975. CAILLOIS, Roger. *Les estampes*, Éd. Yves Rivière, Arts et Métiers Graphiques.

1977. DE VREE, Freddy. *Zao Wou-Ki*, Éd. Kunstforum, Schelderode, Belgium (Kunstpocket in Flemish).

1978. VALLIER, Dora. *Zao Wou-Ki, en torno al gesto*, Ed. Polígrafa, Barcelona.

LEYMARIE, Jean. *Zao Wou-Ki*; documentation by Françoise Marquet; Éd. Hier et Demain, Paris; Ed. Polígrafa, Barcelona; Ed. Rizzoli, New York.

1980. MICHAUX, Henri. *Zao Wou-Ki, encres*, and a dialogue with Françoise Marquet; Éd. Cercle d'Art, Paris.

1981. DE VREE, Freddy. *Zao Wou-Ki*, Éd. Kunstforum, Kunstpocket in French.

1986. LEYMARIE, Jean. *Zao Wou-Ki*; documentation by Françoise Marquet; Éd. Cercle d'Art, Paris; Ed. Polígrafa, Barcelona.

1988. ROY, Claude. *Zao Wou-Ki*; Collection Les grands peintres, Éd. Cercle d'Art, Paris.

ABADIE, Daniel and CONTENSOU, Martine. *Zao Wou-Ki*; Collection Les Maîtres de l'art, Éd. Ars Mundi.

NOËL, Bernard. *Zao Wou-Ki, Encres*; Ed. La Librairie Seguier-Archimbaud, Paris.

WOU-KI, Zao. *Autoportrait*; Éd. Fayard, Paris.

BOOKS ILLUSTRATED BY ZAO WOU-KI

1950. MICHAUX, Henri. *Lecture par Henri Michaux de 8 lithographies de Zao Wou-Ki*. Euros et Robert Godet, Paris.

1957. CHAR, René. *Les compagnons dans le jardin*, colour engravings, Broder, Paris.

1962. MALRAUX, André. *La Tentation de l'Occident*. 10 colour lithographs; Les Bibliophiles Comtois, Paris.

JUIN, Hubert. *Les terrasses de jade*. 4 colour engravings. La Source, Paris.

1965. SAINT-JOHN PERSE. *Œuvre poétique*. 8 watercolours reproduced in colour. Rombaldi, Paris.

1966. RIMBAUD, Arthur. *Les illuminations*. 8 watercolours reproduced in colour. Le Club Français du livre, Paris.

1967. RIMBAUD, Arthur. *Les illuminations*. 8 original colour engravings. Le Club Français du livre, Paris.

1971. LESCURE, Jean. *L'étang*. 8 colour engravings. Galanis, Paris (selected in 1973 by the French book and graphic arts Committee as one of the "50 beautiful books of 1972").

POUND, Ezra. *Cantos Pisan*. 8 colour engravings. Belfond, Paris.

FRANÇOIS, Jocelyne. *Feu de Roue*. 1 colour lithograph. Fata Morgana, Montpellier.

KOBLER, Arnold. *Gerald Cramer, Trente ans d'activité*. Prints by Arp, Braque, Calder, Chadwick, Chagall, Dunoyer de Segonzac, Max Ernst, Marino Marini, Henri Matisse, André Masson, Joan Miró, Henry Moore, Picasso, Siqueiros, Jacques Villon and Zao Wou-Ki. Cramer, Geneva.

1974. LAUDE, Jean. *En attendant un jour de fête*. 1 etching. Fata Morgana, Montpellier.

LAPORTE, Roger. *Une migration*. Letter-preface by René Char, frontspiece by Zao Wou-Ki. 1 original etching. Fata Morgana, Montpellier.

CHAR, René. *Le monde de l'art n'est pas le monde du pardon*. 6 colour lithographs: Miró, Lam, Szènes, Vieira da Silva, Charbonnier, Zao Wou-Ki. Maeght, Paris.

1975. CAILLOIS, Roger. *Randonnée*. 5 colour etchings illustrating a text by Roger Caillois. Yves Rivière, Paris.

CADIEU, Martine. *La mémoire amoureuse*. Letter-preface by René Char, frontispiece by Zao Wou-Ki, 1 original etching. Rougerie, Limoges.

San Lazzaro et ses amis. 9 colour lithographs: Max Bill, Calder, Chagall, Max Ernst, Hartung, Miró, Moore, Sutherland and Zao Wou-Ki. Éd. XXᵉ Siècle, Paris.

1976. GALL, Christian. *Bocage pour les allusions à Brève*. With one black-and-white print. Éd. Saint-Germain-des-Prés, Paris.

CAILLOIS, Roger. *À la gloire de l'image*. With 15 colour lithographs. La Polígrafa, Barcelona.

BOUDAILLE, Georges; LESCURE, Jean; PARMELIN, Hélène. *Hommage à Federico Fellini* (Illustrations by) Corneille, Kijno, Labisse, Lindström, Messagier, Pignon, Prassinos, Singier, Zao Wou-Ki. Grégory, Rome.

1977. *Hommages aux Prix Nobel*. Portfolio of 33 artists. Galerie Börjeson, Malmö.

1978. SENGHOR, Léopold Sédar. *Élégie pour Jean-Marie*. With 4 colour lithographs. Éd. du Regard, Geneva.

1981. JACOTTET, Phillipe. *Beauregard*. With 5 colour engravings. Maeght, Paris.

JAMME, F.A. *L'ombre des biens à venir*. With 2 black-and-white engravings. Thierry Bouchard.

GASPAR, Lorand. *Genèse*. With three black-and-white engravings. Thierry Bouchard.

1985. GASPAR, Lorand. *Journaux de voyages*. Ink drawings by Zao Wou-Ki. Éd. Le Calligraphe, Paris.

1986. MICHAUX, Henri. *En occident, le jardin d'une femme indienne*, 25 copies with an original India ink drawing. Éd. L'Ire des vents, Paris.

1988. PEYRÉ, Yves. *L'Évidence de la nuit*. 4 engravings in black and white, 90 copies. Éd. J. T. Quentin, Geneva.

ONE-MAN EXHIBITIONS

1941. Chino-Soviet Association, Chung-King.

1947. Ta-Hsin Department Store, Shanghai.

1949. Galerie Creuze, Paris. Catalogue foreword by Bernard Dorival.

1951. Galerie Klipstein, Berne: Paintings.
Galerie Pierre, Paris: Paintings.
Galerie La Hune, Paris: Drawings and engravings. Presentation of *Lecture par Henri Michaux de huit lithographies de Zao Wou-Ki.*
Galerie Laya, Geneva.

1952. Galerie Feigel, Basel: Paintings.
Mainstreet Gallery, Chicago: Paintings and watercolours.
Hanover Gallery, London: Paintings, Catalogue foreword by Henri Michaux (Translation by Sylvie Beach).
Cadby-Birch Gallery, New York: Paintings. Catalogue foreword by Henri Michaux (Translation by Sylvie Beach).
Cadby-Birch Gallery, New York: Paintings. Catalogue foreword by Henri Michaux (Translation by Sylvie Beach).
Galerie Pierre, Paris: Paintings.
Galerie de la Vieille Fontaine, Lausanne.
White Gallery, Washington.

1953. Galerie La Hune, Paris: Watercolours and lithographs.
Galerie Klipstein, Berne: Lithographs.
Galleria dell'Obelisco, Rome: Paintings.
Galerie Gerald Cramer, Geneva: Engravings.
Galerie Otto Stangl, Munich: Watercolours.

1954. Cadby-Birch Gallery, New York: Paintings.
Galerie Otto Stangl, Munich: Watercolours.
Galleria del Sole, Milan: Paintings.

1955. Fine Arts Museum, Cincinatti: Lithographs and engravings.
Galerie Pierre, Paris: Paintings.

1956. Kleemann Gallery, New York: Paintings and watercolours.
Galerie Lucien Blanc, Aix-en-Provence.
Galerie La Hune, Paris: Watercolours.
Galerie du Capitole, Lausanne: Paintings.

1957. Galerie de France, Paris: Paintings.
Galerie Müller, Berne.
Galerie Henning, Halle.

1958. Kootz Gallery, New York.

1959. Kootz Gallery, New York.

1960. Galerie Ketterer, Stuttgart.
Galerie de France, Paris.
Mala Gallery, Ljubljana: retrospective group of engravings.

1961. Kootz Gallery, New York.
Tokyo Gallery, Tokyo.
Art O Gallery, Landwerlin, Strasbourg: Engravings.

1962. Exhibition Hall, Ateneo de Madrid: Paintings, watercolours and lithographs.
Galería Liceo, Córdoba: The same exhibition.
Galerie La Hune, Paris: Recent gouaches. Presentation of by André Malraux's *La tentation de l'Occident,* published by the Comtois Bibliophiles and illustrated with lithographs by Zao Wou-Ki.
Gallerie Tornabuoni, Florence: Engravings.

1963. Galerie de France, Paris.
Redfern Gallery, London.
Galerie Parti-Pris, Grenoble: Oils, drawings, watercolours and engravings.

1964. Galerie La Pochade, Paris: "Dix ans de gravures».
Kootz Gallery, New York: Recent paintings.
Massachusetts Institute of Technology, Hayden Gallery, Cambridge (United States): Retrospective.
Galerie de France, Paris.

1965. Folkwang Museum, Essen: Retrospective.
Graphische Sammlung Albertina, Vienna: Watercolours and engravings.
Forum Stadpark, Graz: Watercolours and engravings.
Kootz Gallery, New York.

1966. Maison de la Culture, Caen: Paintings.
Galleria La Bussola, Turin: Paintings, engravings and lithographs.
Galerie Géo-Michel, Brussels: Engravings and lithographs.

1967. Holst Halvorsen Gallery, Oslo: Drawings and watercolours.
Christiansands Kunstforening, Christiansand (Norway). Stavanger Kunstforening, Stavanger (Norway).
Galerie de France, París: Paintings and watercolours.

1968. Frank Perls Gallery, Los Angeles: Paintings and engravings.
Museum of Art, San Francisco: Paintings, engravings and lithographs.

1969. Galerie de l'Angle aigu, Brussels: Watercolours and lithographs.
Galerie Saint-Michel, Bordeaux.
Galerie de Montreal, Montreal.
Musée d'Art contemporain, Montreal: Retrospective.
Musée du Québec: Retrospective.

1970. Galerie Gerald Cramer, Geneva: Watercolours, illustrated books and engravings.
Galerie Argos, Nantes: Paintings and watercolours.
Internationale Sommerakademie für Bildende Kunst, Salzbourg.
Galerie de France, Paris.
Palais des Beaux-Arts, Charleroi. Retrospective.
Galerie At Home, Toulouse.

1971. Galerie Philippe Ducastel, Avignon: Paintings, watercolours and lithographs.
Galerie Candillac, Bordeaux: Paintings, watercolours and lithographs.
Galerie Pierre Hautot, Paris: Engravings and lithographs.
Galerie Municipale, Esch-sur-Alzette (Luxembourg): Paintings, watercolours and engraving work.

1972. Galerie Maurel, Nîmes: Paintings and engravings.
Kunst Forum, Schelderode: Paintings.
Galerie de France, Paris: Wash drawings, with sculptures by May Zao.

1973. Galerie Protée, Toulouse: Paintings and wash drawings.
Musée d'Art et d'Histoire, Neuchâtel.
Galerie Melisa, Lausanne.
Observatoire de Genèva, Sauverny: Lithographs and engravings.
Chapelle du Parage, Les Arcs.
Galería Carl Van der Voort, Ibiza: Watercolours and drawings.
Galerie Synthèse, Antwerp: Engraving work and wash drawings.
Galerie Ducastel, Avignon: Engraving work and wash drawings.

1974. Galerie Diprove, Lisbon: Paintings, engraving work and wash drawings.
Galerie Diprove, Oporto: The same exhibition.
Maison des Arts et Lettres, Sochaux: Wash paintings.
Galerie Kutter, Luxembourg: Paintings and watercolours, wash drawings and lithographs.
Heimeshoff Galerie, Essen: Paintings, watercolours and engravings.
Galerie Nicolas, Amsterdam: Paintings, watercolours and wash drawings.
Galerie Bruck, Luxembourg: engraving work.

1975. Salon des Beaux-Arts, Centre Culturel de Creil: "Hommage à Zao Wou-Ki" (15 paintings).
Galerie de l'Ours, Bourges: Watercolours and engraving work.
Galerie Art et Matière, Grenoble: Watercolours and engraving work.
Galerie 31, Strasbourg: engraving work.
Fondation Veranneman, Kruishouten (Belgium): Large formats; and four sculptures by May Zao.

Galerie de France, Paris: "1971-1975". Catalogue foreword by René Char.
Galerie ABCD, Paris: Engraving work.

Delta International Art Center, Beirut: Catalogue foreword by Marwann Hoss.
Galerie ACB, Geneva: Illustrated books, watercolours and engraving work.
Maison de la Culture, Saint-Étienne: 20 paintings, watercolours engraving work and sculptures by May Zao. Catalogue foreword by Maurice Allemand.
Galerie Nieuwe Weg, Doorn: Engraving work.
Galerie Nouvelles Images, Lombreuil: Drawings and engraving work.

1976. Galerie Ducastel, Avignon.
Galerie Pro Arte, Mulhouse.
Librairie Fontaine, Paris: Recent engraving work.
Galerie Protée, Toulouse: Paintings, watercolours and wash drawings.
Galerie Jivo, Vanesborg (Sweden): Engraving work by Zao Wou-Ki and Soulages.

1977. Fuji Television Gallery, Tokyo. Catalogue foreword by Tamon Miki and Henri Michaux.

1978. Hôtel de Ville, Châteauroux: 40 engravings; Municipal Library, Châteauroux: *A la gloire de l'image*, by Roger Caillois, illustrated by Zao Wou-Ki.
Callerihauset, Copenhagen: Zao Wou-Ki Poetisk-Grafik.
Galería Joan Prats, Barcelona: *Entorno al gesto*, catalogue foreword by Dora Vallier.
París, FIAC 1978: Atelier Lacourrière et Frélaut; Galerie de France.

1979. Bibliothèque Nationale, Paris: Engraving work, retrospective, Catalogue foreword by Françoise Woimant and Claude Roy.
Galerie Kutter, Luxembourg.
Galería de Site, Alicante, Catalogue foreword by Dora Vallier.
Galerie Madoura, Vallauris.
Centre Culturel du Parvis, Tarbes.

1980. Palais des Beaux-Arts, Charleroi: «Grands Tableaux», catalogue foreword by Robert Rousseau.
Musée de l'État, Luxembourg: Catalogue foreword by Jean-Luc Koltz.
Galerie Kutter, Luxembourg.
Galtung Gallery, Oslo.
Galerie de France, Paris: "Encres de Chine". Text by Henri Michaux.
Dialogue with Françoise Marquet, Paris: Éditions Cercle d'Art.
Printmakers Art Gallery, Taipei: Catalogue foreword by Yuan Tch-sin, Lee Shi-Chi and Tou Yin-Chin.
Châteauneuf-du-Pape, "Grands formats", castle cellars.
Pierre Matisse Gallery, New York: catalogue foreword by I. M. Pei.
Galerie Protée, Toulouse.
Théâtre de Privas, Centre d'Art et de Loisir, Privas.
Information Gallery under the auspices of the National Cultural Committee and the French Embassy in Tunisia, Tunis: Catalogue foreword by Lorand Gaspar.

1981. Singer Museum Concertzaal, Laren (Holland).
French Institute, Athens: "Michaux et Zao Wou-Ki".
Printmakers Art Gallery, Taipei.
Grand Palais, Paris. Catalogue foreword by Jean Leymarie and François Cheng.
Fuji Television Gallery, Tokyo: India ink drawings.

1982. Fukuoka City Museum, Fukuoka: Catalogue foreword by Jean Leymarie and François Cheng. Éd. The Society for International Cultural Exchange.
Tokyo Nihonbashi Art Gallery, Tokyo. The same catalogue.
Fukui Prefectoral Museum, Fukui. The same catalogue.
Kyoto National Museum of Modern Art, Kyoto. The same catalogue.
Kamakura Museum of Modern Art, Kamakura: The same catalogue.
Hong-Kong Arts Center, Hong-Kong: Catalogue foreword by Jean Leymarie and François Cheng.
National Museum of Modern Art, Singapore. Catalogue foreword by Jean Leymarie and François Cheng.
Bibliothèque Municipale, Vichy: Catalogue foreword by Claude Roy.

1983. The National Museum of History, Taipei. Catalogue foreword by H.T. Ho, M.K. Yao, Z. Kuo and W.T. Liu.
Tai-Nan Cultural Centre: The same catalogue.
Prefecture Library, Tai-Chung: The same catalogue.
Musée Ingres, Montauban: Catalogue foreword by Geneviève Bonnefois and Pierre Barousse.
Fine Arts Museum, Pekin: Catalogue forewords by Wu Zuo-ren and Yu-Feng.
Zyejiang Academy of Fine Arts, Hang-Chou: The same catalogue.
Espace des Cordeliers, Châteauroux.

1984. Galerie Jan Krugier, Geneva: Catalogue foreword by Henri Michaux.
Galerie Patrice Trigano, Paris.
Galerie de France, Paris. Catalogue foreword by Georges Duby.

1985. Maison de la Culture, La Rochelle.
Galerie Editart-D. Blanco, Geneva: Engravings.
Galerie Artcurial, Paris: Engravings.

1986. Pierre Matisse Gallery: New York: Recent paintings. Catalogue foreword by François Jacob.
French Cultural Centre, Rome: India ink drawings. Exhibition organised by Jean Leymarie, Paul Bedarida and the AFAA (Association Française d'Action Artistique); catalogue foreword by Jean Leymarie, Henri Michaux and Lorand Gaspar.
Galerie de France, Paris: Présentation of the *Triptyque 280×1000 cm 1985* before its installation in Raffles City, Singapore. Architect: I.M. Pei.
Galerie Protée, Toulouse: Paintings and watercolours.
Artothèque de la Ville de Toulouse: Engravings.
Galerie La Prévote, Aix-en-Provence, as part of the Aix-en-Provence music festival.

1987. Galerie La Loggia, Bologne: The same exhibition as in Rome.
Luxembourg: Paintings and watercolours. Catalogue foreword by Françoise Marquet.
Fuji Television Gallery, Tokyo: Recent paintings. Catalogue foreword by Junji Itô.
Galerie-Librairie Mollat, Bordeaux: "Encres", exhibition organised in conjunction with Éditions Cercle d'Art.

1988. Galerie Lacourière-Frelaut, Paris: India ink drawings, watercolours engravings.
Galerie Jan Krugier, Geneva: Recent paintings. Catalogue foreword by Jean Leymarie.
Artcurial, Paris: Retrospective; catalogue foreword by Pierre Schneider.
FIAC, Artcurial stand: Recent large formats; catalogue foreword by Pierre Schneider.
Musée de Metz.

ILLUSTRATIONS

1. *Wedding.* 1941. Oil on board, 8¾×7½ in. (22×19 cm). Lan-Lan Collection, Paris.

2. *Landscape.* 1949. Oil on tablex, 15×18 in. (38×46 cm). Private collection, Paris.

1

3. *Arezzo.* 1950. Oil on canvas, 36¼×39½ in. (92×100 cm).
Henri Michaux Collection, Paris.

4. *Sunlit Pavilion.* 1954-1955. Oil on canvas, 63¾×51¼ in. (162×130 cm).
    Museo de Arte Moderna, Rio de Janeiro.

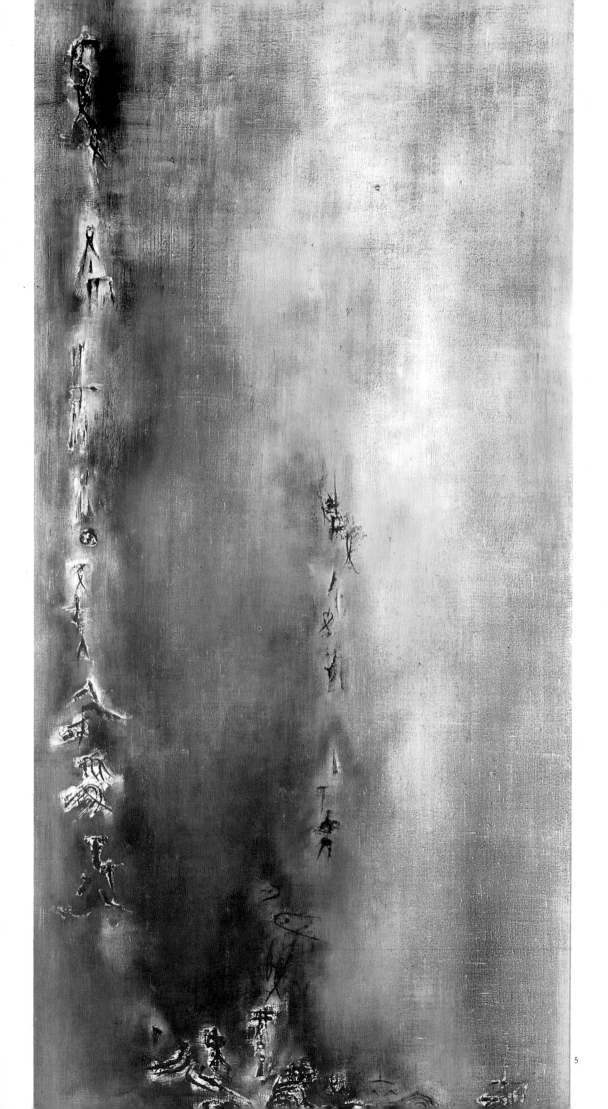

5

5. *Wind.* 1954. Oil on canvas, 76¾×34¼ in. (195×87 cm).
   Musée National d'Art Moderne, Paris.

6. *Before the Storm.* 1955. Oil on canvas, 36¼×28¾ in. (92×73 cm).
   The Tate Gallery, London.

7. *Black Multitude.* 1955. Oil on canvas, 45¾×35 in. (116×89 cm).
   Museum of Art, Carnegie Institute, Pittsburgh.

8. *The River.* 1956. Oil on canvas, 37½×39½ in. (95×100 cm).
   The artist's collection.

9. *Stele for a Friend.* 1956. Oil on canvas, 63¾×44½ in. (162×113 cm).
   Otto Stangl Galerie, Munich.

10. *The Night Stirs.* 1956. Oil on canvas, 76¾×51¼ in. (195×130 cm).
    The Art Institute of Chicago. Mrs Samuel M. Kootz Donation.

11. *Composition.* 1957. Oil on canvas, 78¾×118 in. (200×300 cm).
Nagaoka Museum of Contemporary Art, Nagaoka, Japan.

12. *1957*. Oil on canvas, 25½×18 in. (65×46 cm).
    Hans Hartung Collection, Paris.

13. *And the Earth Had no Form.* 1957. Oil on canvas, 78¾×63¾ in.
    (200×162 cm).
    Private collection, Switzerland.

14. *Mistral.* 1957. Oil on canvas, 51¼×76¾ in. (130×195 cm).
The Solomon R. Guggenheim Museum, New York.

14

15. *Painting.* 1958. Oil on canvas, 28¾×39½ in. (73×100 cm).
Mrs Lester Dana Collection, Boston.

15

16. *15-1-59*. Oil on canvas, 51¼×38¼ in. (130×97 cm).
Private collection, Paris.

17. *21-14-59*. Oil on canvas, 51¼×63¾ in. (130×162 cm).
    Private collection, Paris.

18. *6-1-60*. Oil on canvas, 51¼×76¾ in. (130×195 cm).
Private collection, Paris.

19. *2-11-59*. Oil on canvas, 51¼×38¼ in. (130×97 cm).
   Private collection, New York.

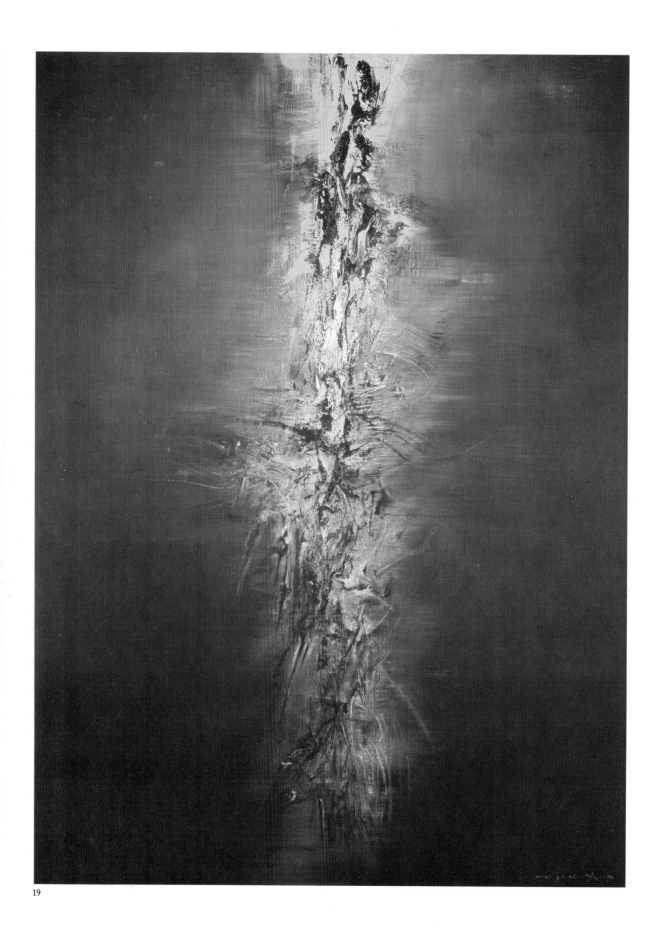

20. *1-3-60*. Oil on canvas, 63¾×78¾ in. (162×200 cm).
Société des Compteurs Schlumberger Collection, Paris.

21. *14-6-61*. Oil on canvas, 31¾×25½ in. (81×65 cm).
Mr and Mrs John Cowles Collection, New York.

22. *27-5-61*. Oil on canvas, 39½×28¾ in. (100×73 cm).
Private collection, United States.

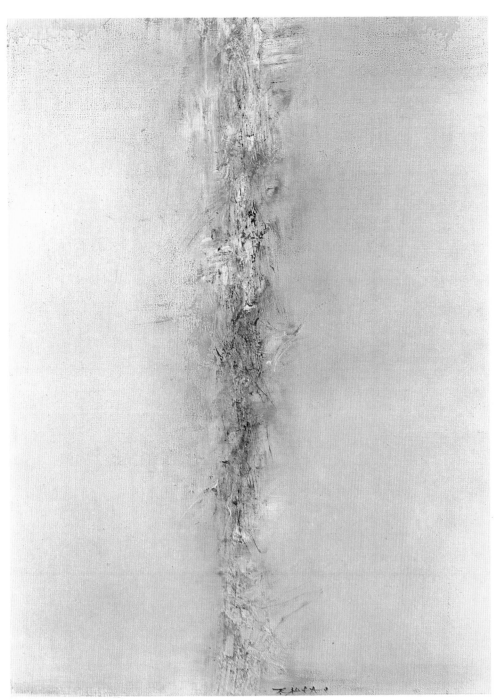

23. *14-4-62*. Oil on canvas, 31¾×51¼ in. (81×130 cm).
Private collection, Paris.

23

24. *17-3-63*. Oil on canvas, 51¼×38¼ in. (130×97 cm).
     Private collection, Le Vésinet.

24

25. *16-6-64*. Oil on canvas, 57½×44¾ in. (146×114 cm).
Cuyahoya Saving Association Collection, Cleveland, Ohio.

26. *29-1-64*. Oil on canvas, 102½×78¾ in. (260×200 cm).
Private collection, Paris.

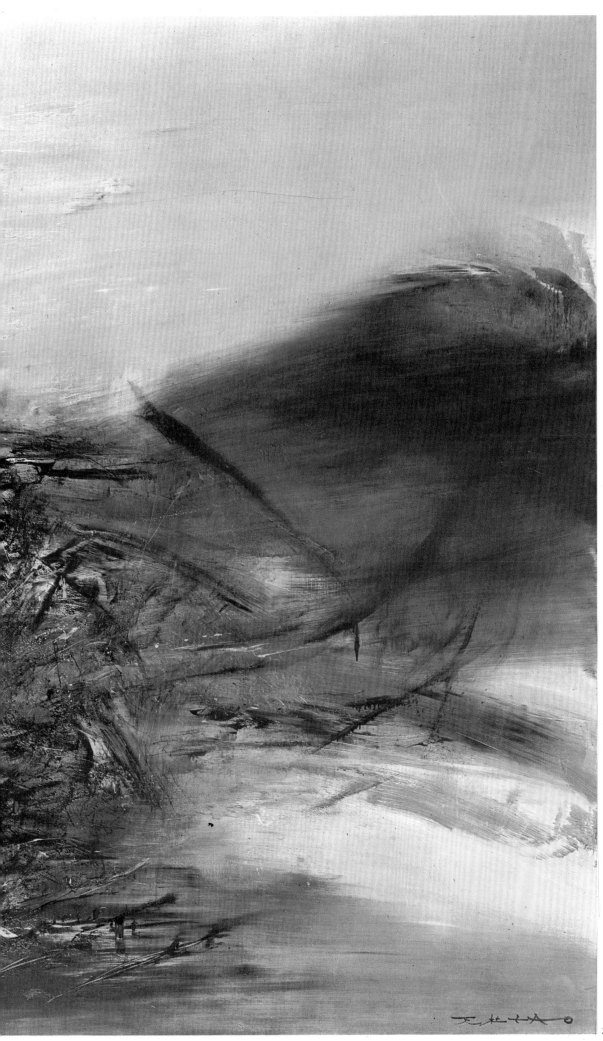

27. *Homage to
Edgar Varèse. 25-10-64.*
Oil on canvas,
100½×136 in.
(255×345 cm).
Private collection,
Paris.

28. *3-11-68*. Oil on canvas, 76¾×51¼ in. (195×130 cm).
Private collection, Paris.

29. *1-4-68*. Oil on canvas, 73¾×51¼ in. (195×130 cm).
     The artist's collection.

30. *5-9-69*. Oil on canvas, 73¾×51¼ in. (195×130 cm).
Gana Gallery, Seoul.

31. *3-4-60/1-2-69*. Oil on canvas, 73¾×51¼ in. (195×130 cm).
     Galerie de France, Paris.

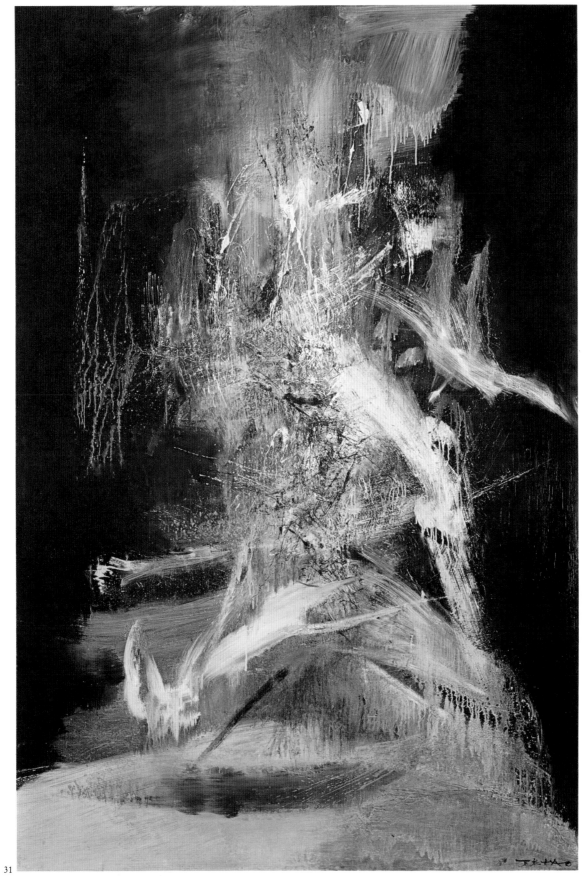

32. *18-12-69*. Oil on canvas, 45¾×35 in. (116×89 cm).
The artist's collection.

33. *6-10-71*. Oil on canvas, 76¾×51¼ in. (195×130 cm).
Musée Bertrand, Châteauroux.

33

34. *25-5-70*. Oil on canvas, 59×63¾ in. (150×162 cm).
Private collection, Lisbon.

34

35. *2-10-66/8-2-71*. Oil on canvas, ⌀ 21¾ in. (55 cm).
Private collection, Paris.

35

36. *10-9-72. May, in Memoriam.* (14-11-30/10-3-72.) Oil on canvas, 78¾×206½ in. (200×525 cm).
Musée National d'Art Moderne, Paris.

37. *14-7-61/28-1-71*. Oil on canvas, 78¾×63¾ in. (200×162 cm).

38. *19-11-71.* Oil on canvas, 78¾×63¾ in. (200×162 cm).
French Consulate Collection, Hong Kong (lent by the Fonds National d'Art Contemporain, Paris).

39. *9-5-59/8-1-71*. Oil on canvas, 78¾×63¾ in. (200×162 cm). Museo de Arte Contemporáneo Rufino Tamayo, Mexico.

40. *10-11-58/30-12-70*. Oil on canvas, 51¼×76¾ in. (130×195 cm).
Private collection, Mexico.

41. *13-9-73*. Oil on canvas, 78¾×63¾ in. (200×162 cm).
Musée Ingres, Montauban.

42. *10-1-74*. Oil on canvas, 76¾×51¼ in. (195×130 cm).
Bibliothèque Préfectorale, Tai-chung (Taiwan).

43. *1-10-73*. Oil on canvas, 102½×78¾ in. (260×200 cm).

44. *10-3-73*. Oil on canvas, 102½×78¾ in. (260×200 cm).
Musée National d'Art Moderne, Osaka.

45. *28-8-74.* Oil on canvas, 36¼×28¾ in. (92×73 cm).
     J. R. Arnaud Collection, Paris.

46. *14-12-66/20-4-74*. Oil on canvas, ⌀ 39½ in. (100 cm).
Sin-May Zao Collection, Paris.

47. *2-3-74*. Oil on canvas, 63¾×51¼ in. (162×130 cm).
The artist's collection.

46

48. *3-12-74*. Oil on canvas, 98½×102½ in. (250×260 cm).
Fonds National d'Art Contemporain, Paris.

49. *1-12-75*. Oil on canvas,
44¾×57½ in. (114×146 cm).
Thyssen-Bornemisza Collection,
Castagnola (Switzerland).

50. *13-1-76*. Oil on canvas, 59×63¾ in. (150×162 cm).
Pierre Matisse Gallery, New York.

51. *1-4-76. Triptych. Homage to André Malraux.* Oil on canvas, 78¾×206½ in. (200×524 cm).
The Hakone Open-Air Museum, Hakone.

52. *14-11-76*. Oil on canvas, 102½×78¾ in. (260×200 cm).
Pierre Matisse Gallery, New York.

53. *15-4-77*. Oil on canvas, 78¾×63¾ in. (200×162 cm).
Eillen and I.M. Pei Collection, New York.

54. *10-2-76*. Oil on canvas, 32×39½ in. (81×100 cm).
Galerie Birch, Copenhagen.

55. *10-3-76*. Oil on canvas, 76¾×38¼ in. (195×97 cm).
Mr and Mrs Kanichiro Ishibashi Collection, Tokyo.

56. *27-6-79*. Oil on canvas, 51¼×76¾ in. (130×195 cm).
Pierre Matisse Gallery, New York.

57. *21-4-80*. Oil on canvas, 102½×78¾ in. (260×200 cm).
Galerie Aix, Stockholm.

56

58. *24-11-80*. Triptych. Oil on canvas, 78¾×206½ in. (200×525 cm).
Pierre Matisse Gallery, New York.

59. *1-4-81*. Oil on canvas, 102½×88½ in. (260×225 cm).
Musée National d'Art Moderne, Paris.

60. *27-8-82*. Triptych. Oil on canvas, 78¾×206½ in. (200×525 cm).
The Hakone Open-Air Museum Collection, Hakone.

61. *1-5-82*. Oil on canvas, 98½×102½ in. (250×260 cm).

62. *4-1-82*. Oil on canvas, 102½×78¾ in. (260×200 cm).
Total, Compagnie Française des Pétroles Collection, Paris.

63. *1-6-83*. Oil on canvas, 78¾×63¾ in. (200×162 cm).

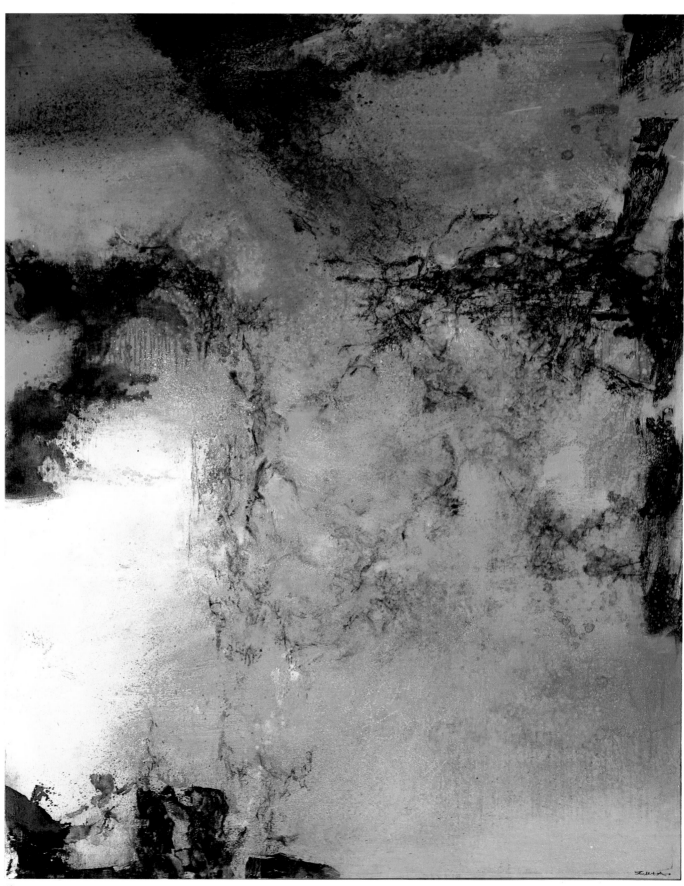

64. *5-3-75/7-1-85*. Oil on canvas, 98½×102½ in. (250×260 cm).
The artist's collection.

65. *10-2-84*. Oil on canvas, 78¾×63¾ in. (200×162 cm).
Galerie Jan Krugier, Geneva.

66. *1-12-82/24-1-84*. Oil on canvas, 78¾×63¾ in. (200×162 cm).
 Galerie de France, Paris.

67. *20-3-84*. Oil on canvas, 102½×78¾ in. (260×200 cm).
 Fonds National d'Art Contemporain, Paris.

68. *2-10-84*. Oil on canvas, 57½×45 in. (146×114 cm).
    Galerie Jan Krugier, Geneva.

69. *10-3-85*. Oil on canvas, 38¼×76¾ in. (97×195 cm).
Michèle and Antoine Riboud Collection, Paris.

70. *4-4-85*. Oil on canvas, 38¼×76¾ in. (97×195 cm).
Pierre Matisse Gallery, New York.

70

71. *18-3-85.* Oil on canvas, 63¾×59 in. (162×150 cm). Pierre Matisse Gallery, New York.

72

72.   *21-1-85*. Oil on canvas, 76¾×45 in. (195×114 cm).
      Galerie de France, Paris.

73.   *15-4-86*. Oil on canvas, 63¾×59 in. (162×150 cm).
      Artcurial, Paris.

74. *June-October*. 1985. Triptych. Oil on canvas, 110½×393½ in. (280×1000 cm).
Raffles City Collection, Singapore. Architect: I.M. Pei.

74

75. *2-12-87*. Oil on canvas, 102½×78¾ in. (260×200 cm).
    Artcurial, Paris.

76. *15-5-88*. Oil on canvas, 102½×78¾ in. (260×200 cm).
Artcurial, Paris.

77. *Triptych.* 1987-1988. Oil on canvas, 78¾×191½ in. (200×486 cm).
The artist's collection.

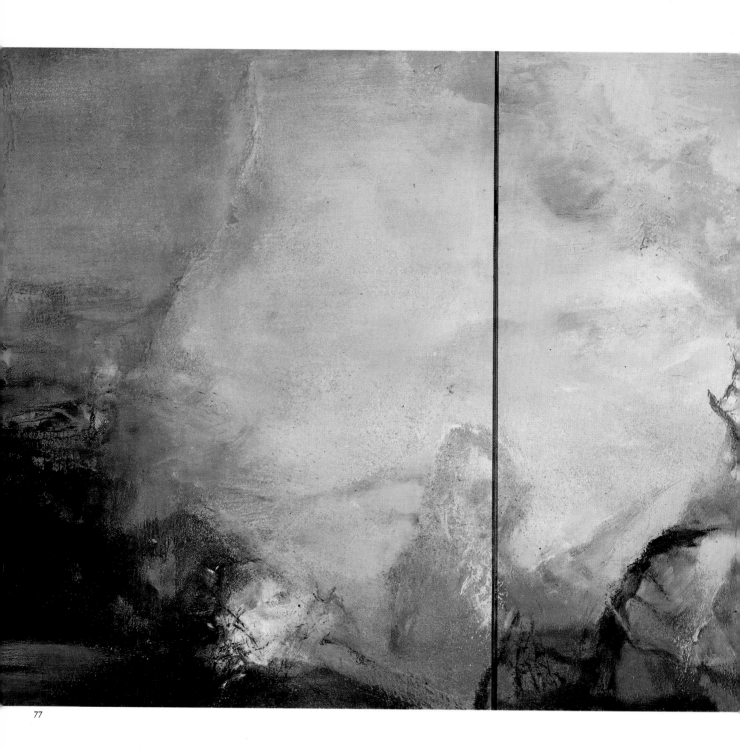

77

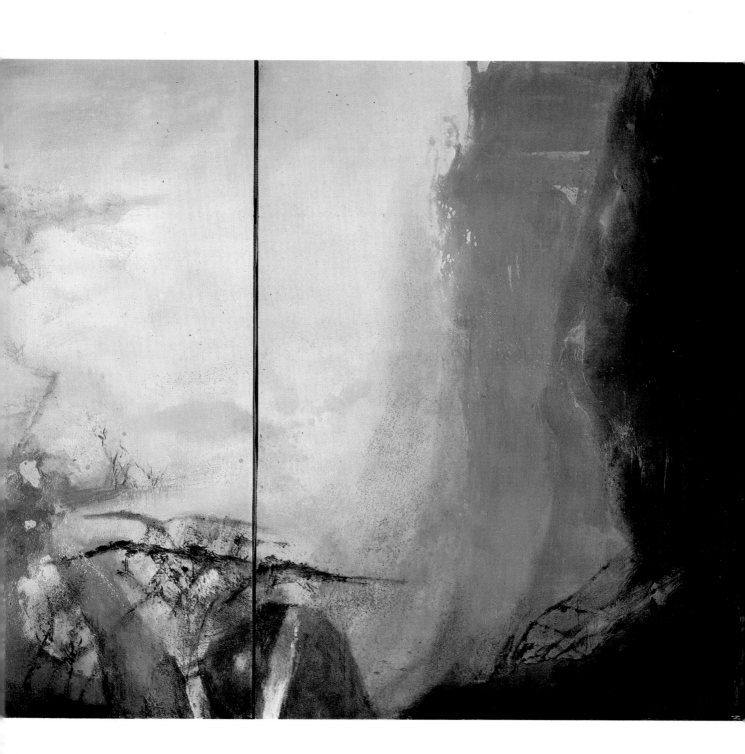

78. *1-6-88*. Oil on canvas, 78¾×63¾ in. (200×162 cm).
Artcurial, Paris.

LIST OF WORKS

1. *Wedding.* 1941. Oil on board, 8¾×7½ in. (22×19 cm). Lan-Lan Collection, Paris.

2. *Landscape.* 1949. Oil on tablex, 15×18 in. (38×46 cm). Private collection, Paris.

3. *Arezzo.* 1950. Oil on canvas, 36¼×39½ in. (92×100 cm). Henri Michaux Collection, Paris.

4. *Sunlit Pavilion.* 1954-1955. Oil on canvas, 63¾×51¼ in. (162×130 cm). Museo de Arte Moderna, Rio de Janeiro.

5. *Wind.* 1954. Oil on canvas, 76¾×34¼ in. (195×87 cm). Musée National d'Art Moderne, Paris.

6. *Before the Storm.* 1955. Oil on canvas, 36¼×28¾ in. (92×73 cm). The Tate Gallery, London.

7. *Black Multitude.* 1955. Oil on canvas, 45¾×35 in. (116×89 cm). Museum of Art, Carnegie Institute, Pittsburgh.

8. *The River.* 1956. Oil on canvas, 37½×39½ in. (95×100 cm). The artist's collection.

9. *Stele for a Friend.* 1956. Oil on canvas, 63¾×44½ in. (162×113 cm). Otto Stangl Galerie, Munich.

10. *The Night Stirs.* 1956. Oil on canvas, 76¾×51¼ in. (195×130 cm). The Art Institute of Chicago. Mrs Samuel M. Kootz Donation.

11. *Composition.* 1957. Oil on canvas, 78¾×118 in. (200×300 cm). Nagaoka Museum of Contemporary Art, Nagaoka, Japan.

12. *1957.* Oil on canvas, 25½×18 in. (65×46 cm). Hans Hartung Collection, Paris.

13. *And the Earth Had no Form.* 1957. Oil on canvas, 78¾×63¾ in. (200×162 cm). Private collection, Switzerland.

14. *Mistral.* 1957. Oil on canvas, 51¼×76¾ in. (130×195 cm). The Solomon R. Guggenheim Museum, New York.

15. *Painting.* 1958. Oil on canvas, 28¾×39½ in. (73×100 cm). Mrs Lester Dana Collection, Boston.

16. *15-1-59.* Oil on canvas, 51¼×38¼ in. (130×97 cm). Private collection, Paris.

17. *21-14-59.* Oil on canvas, 51¼×63¾ in. (130×162 cm). Private collection, Paris.

18. *6-1-60.* Oil on canvas, 51¼×76¾ in. (130×195 cm). Private collection, Paris.

19. *2-11-59.* Oil on canvas, 51¼×38¼ in. (130×97 cm). Private collection, New York.

20. *1-3-60.* Oil on canvas, 63¾×78¾ in. (162×200 cm). Société des Compteurs Schlumberger Collection, Paris.

21. *14-6-61.* Oil on canvas, 31¾×25½ in. (81×65 cm). Mr and Mrs John Cowles Collection, New York.

22. *27-5-61.* Oil on canvas, 39½×28¾ in. (100×73 cm). Private collection, United States.

23. *14-4-62.* Oil on canvas, 31¾×51¼ in. (81×130 cm). Private collection, Paris.

24. *17-3-63.* Oil on canvas, 51¼×38¼ in. (130×97 cm). Private collection, Le Vésinet.

25. *16-6-64.* Oil on canvas, 57½×44¾ in. (146×114 cm). Cuyahoya Saving Association Collection, Cleveland, Ohio.

26. *29-1-64.* Oil on canvas, 102½×78¾ in. (260×200 cm). Private collection, Paris.

27. *Homage to Edgar Varèse. 25-10-64.* Oil on canvas, 100½×136 in. (255×345 cm). Private collection, Paris.

28. *3-11-68.* Oil on canvas, 76¾×51¼ in. (195×130 cm). Private collection, Paris.

29. *1-4-68.* Oil on canvas, 73¾×51¼ in. (195×130 cm). The artist's collection.

30. *5-9-69.* Oil on canvas, 73¾×51¼ in. (195×130 cm). Gana Gallery, Seoul.

31. *3-4-60/1-2-69.* Oil on canvas, 73¾×51¼ in. (195×130 cm). Galerie de France, Paris.

32. *18-12-69.* Oil on canvas, 45¾×35 in. (116×89 cm). The artist's collection.

33. *6-10-71.* Oil on canvas, 76¾×51¼ in. (195×130 cm). Musée Bertrand, Châteauroux.

34. *25-5-70.* Oil on canvas, 59×63¾ in. (150×162 cm). Private collection, Lisbon.

35. *2-10-66/8-2-71.* Oil on canvas, ∅ 21¾ in. (55 cm). Private collection, Paris.

36. *10-9-72. May, in Memoriam.* (14-11-30/10-3-72.) Oil on canvas, 78¾×206½ in. (200×525 cm). Musée National d'Art Moderne, Paris.

37. *14-7-61/28-1-71.* Oil on canvas, 78¾×63¾ in. (200×162 cm).

38. *19-11-71.* Oil on canvas, 78¾×63¾ in. (200×162 cm). French Consulate Collection, Hong Kong (lent by the Fonds National d'Art Contemporain, Paris).

39. *9-5-59/8-1-71.* Oil on canvas, 78¾×63¾ in. (200×162 cm). Museo de Arte Contemporáneo Rufino Tamayo, Mexico.

40. *10-11-58/30-12-70.* Oil on canvas, 51¼×76¾ in. (130×195 cm). Private collection, Mexico.

41. *13-9-73.* Oil on canvas, 78¾×63¾ in. (200×162 cm). Musée Ingres, Montauban.

42. *10-1-74.* Oil on canvas, 76¾×51¼ in. (195×130 cm). Bibliothèque Préfectorale, Tai-chung (Taiwan).

43. *1-10-73.* Oil on canvas, 102½×78¾ in. (260×200 cm).

44. *10-3-73.* Oil on canvas, 102½×78¾ in. (260×200 cm). Musée National d'Art Moderne, Osaka.

45. *28-8-74*. Oil on canvas, 36¼×28¾ in. (92×73 cm). J. R. Arnaud Collection, Paris.

46. *14-12-66/20-4-74*. Oil on canvas, ⊘ 39½ in. (100 cm). Sin-May Zao Collection, Paris.

47. *2-3-74*. Oil on canvas, 63¾×51¼ in. (162×130 cm). The artist's collection.

48. *3-12-74*. Oil on canvas, 98½×102½ in. (250×260 cm). Fonds National d'Art Contemporain, Paris.

49. *1-12-75*. Oil on canvas, 44¾×57½ in. (114×146 cm). Thyssen-Bornemisza Collection, Castagnola (Switzerland).

50. *13-1-76*. Oil on canvas, 59×63¾ in. (150×162 cm). Pierre Matisse Gallery, New York.

51. *1-4-76. Triptych. Homage to André Malraux.* Oil on canvas, 78¾×206½ in. (200×524 cm). The Hakone Open-Air Museum, Hakone.

52. *14-11-76*. Oil on canvas, 102½×78¾ in. (260×200 cm). Pierre Matisse Gallery, New York.

53. *15-4-77*. Oil on canvas, 78¾×63¾ in. (200×162 cm). Eillen and I.M. Pei Collection, New York.

54. *10-2-76*. Oil on canvas, 32×39½ in. (81×100 cm). Galerie Birch, Copenhagen.

55. *10-3-76*. Oil on canvas, 76¾×38¼ in. (195×97 cm). Mr and Mrs Kanichiro Ishibashi Collection, Tokyo.

56. *27-6-79*. Oil on canvas, 51¼×76¾ in. (130×195 cm). Pierre Matisse Gallery, New York.

57. *21-4-80*. Oil on canvas, 102½×78¾ in. (260×200 cm). Galerie Aix, Stockholm.

58. *24-11-80*. Triptych. Oil on canvas, 78¾×206½ in. (200×525 cm). Pierre Matisse Gallery, New York.

59. *1-4-81*. Oil on canvas, 102½×88½ in. (260×225 cm). Musée National d'Art Moderne, Paris.

60. *27-8-82*. Triptych. Oil on canvas, 78¾×206½ in. (200×525 cm). The Hakone Open-Air Museum Collection, Hakone.

61. *1-5-82*. Oil on canvas, 98½×102½ in. (250×260 cm).

62. *4-1-82*. Oil on canvas, 102½×78¾ in. (260×200 cm). Total, Compagnie Française des Pétroles Collection, Paris.

63. *1-6-83*. Oil on canvas, 78¾×63¾ in. (200×162 cm).

64. *5-3-75/7-1-85*. Oil on canvas, 98½×102½ in. (250×260 cm). The artist's collection.

65. *10-2-84*. Oil on canvas, 78¾×63¾ in. (200×162 cm). Galerie Jan Krugier, Geneva.

66. *1-12-82/24-1-84*. Oil on canvas, 78¾×63¾ in. (200×162 cm). Galerie de France, Paris.

67. *20-3-84*. Oil on canvas, 102½×78¾ in. (260×200 cm). Fonds National d'Art Contemporain, Paris.

68. *2-10-84*. Oil on canvas, 57½×45 in. (146×114 cm). Galerie Jan Krugier, Geneva.

69. *10-3-85*. Oil on canvas, 38¼×76¾ in. (97×195 cm). Michèle and Antoine Riboud Collection, Paris.

70. *4-4-85*. Oil on canvas, 38¼×76¾ in. (97×195 cm). Pierre Matisse Gallery, New York.

71. *18-3-85*. Oil on canvas, 63¾×59 in. (162×150 cm). Pierre Matisse Gallery, New York.

72. *21-1-85*. Oil on canvas, 76¾×45 in. (195×114 cm). Galerie de France, Paris.

73. *15-4-86*. Oil on canvas, 63¾×59 in. (162×150 cm). Artcurial, Paris.

74. *June-October*. 1985. Triptych. Oil on canvas, 110½×393½ in. (280×1000 cm). Raffles City Collection, Singapore. Architect: I.M. Pei.

75. *2-12-87*. Oil on canvas, 102½×78¾ in. (260×200 cm). Artcurial, Paris.

76. *15-5-88*. Oil on canvas, 102½×78¾ in. (260×200 cm). Artcurial, Paris.

77. *Triptych*. 1987-1988. Oil on canvas, 78¾×191½ in. (200×486 cm). The artist's collection.

78. *1-6-88*. Oil on canvas, 78¾×63¾ in. (200×162 cm). Artcurial, Paris.